ENDURANCE

ENDURANCE

YOUNG READERS EDITION

MY YEAR IN SPACE
AND HOW I GOT THERE

SCOTT KELLY

WITH

MARGARET LAZARUS DEAN

ADAPTED FOR YOUNG READERS BY

EMILY EASTON

CROWN BOOKS
FOR YOUNG READERS
NEW YORK

TO MY CHILDREN, SAMANTHA AND CHARLOTTE,

FOR THE SACRIFICES THEY HAVE ENDURED

HAVING A DAD WHO WORKS IN SPACE

PART 1

LEARNING
TO FLY

Buzz Aldrin stands beside the U.S. flag during the first moon landing of the Apollo 11 mission as Neil Armstrong takes his picture. July 20, 1969.

INTRODUCTION

When I was a boy, I had a strange recurring daydream. I saw myself stuck in a small space, barely big enough to lie down in. Curled up on the floor, I knew that I would be there for a long time. I couldn't leave, but I didn't mind. There was something about the challenge of living in such a small space that was appealing to me. I felt I had everything I needed and was where I belonged.

One night when I was five, my parents shook Mark and me awake and led us down to the living room to watch a blurry gray image on TV. They explained we were about to see men walking on the moon. I remember hearing the broken voice of Neil Armstrong and trying to believe that he was really walking on the glowing disk I could see out our window.

When I joined NASA's class of 1996 and started getting to know my astronaut classmates, many of us shared the same memory of coming downstairs in our pajamas as little kids to watch the moon landing. Most of us had decided, then and there, to go to space one day. At that time, we were promised that Americans would land on the surface of Mars by 1975. Anything was possible now that we had put a man on the moon. Then NASA (the National Aeronautics and Space Administration) lost most of its funding after the public lost interest in new Apollo missions, and our dreams of space had to be downgraded.

In the years since, NASA has built the International Space Station (ISS), the hardest engineering feat human beings have ever achieved. Getting to Mars and back will be even harder, and I have spent a year in space—longer than it would take to get to Mars—to help answer some of the questions about how we can survive that journey.

1

MY EARLIEST MEMORIES are of the warm summer nights when my mother, Patricia, tried to settle Mark and me to sleep in our house on Mitchell Street in West Orange, New Jersey. It was still light outside, and I could hear the sounds of the neighborhood drifting in through the open windows—older kids yelling, the thumps of basketballs against driveways, the rustling of breezes high in the trees, the faraway sounds of traffic. I remember the feeling of drifting weightless between summer and sleep.

My brother and I were born in 1964. Members of my father's side of our family lived all up and down our block, aunts and uncles and cousins in both directions. The town was separated by a hill. The more well-off lived "up the hill," and we lived "down the hill." I remember waking early in the morning with my brother when we were small, maybe two years old. My parents were sleeping, so we were on our own. We got bored, figured out how to open the back door, and left the house to explore, two toddlers wandering the neighborhood. We made our way to a gas station, where we played in the grease until the owner found us. He knew where we lived and stuck us back in the house without waking my parents. When my mother finally got up and came downstairs, she was confused by the grease all over us. Later that day, the owner came over and told her what had happened.

One afternoon when we were in kindergarten, my mother told us she had an important task for us. She held a white envelope in front of her as if it were a special prize. Mom told us to put the letter in a mailbox directly across the street from our house. But first, she warned us that it wasn't safe to cross in the middle of the street—we could be hit by a car. So we were to walk up to the corner and cross the street there, then walk back to the mailbox on the other side of the street and mail the letter. When our job was done, we needed to take the long way home, walking to the corner to cross again. We promised to follow her instructions.

Two future astronauts playing in the New Jersey snow at almost three years old. December 1966.

Mark and I set off and walked up to the corner. We looked both ways, crossed, and made our way to the mailbox. Mark boosted me up to pull down the heavy blue handle, and I proudly deposited the letter in the slot. With our job complete, it was time to head back home.

"I'm not walking all the way back to the corner," Mark announced. "I'm just going to cross the street right here."

"Mom said we should cross at the corner," I reminded him. "You're going to get hit by a car."

But Mark had made up his mind.

I set off back toward the corner myself, eager to get home and be praised for having followed directions. I reached the corner, crossed, and turned back toward the house. The next thing I heard was car brakes squealing and the thump of a collision. Out of the corner of my eye, I saw something the size and shape of a kid flying up into the air.

Mark sat, dazed, in the middle of the street, while the frantic driver fussed over him. Someone ran for our mother, an ambulance came, and Mark was whisked away to the hospital. I spent the rest of the afternoon and evening with my uncle Joe and his family. I was left at home to worry about my rule-breaking brother, as I was steaming over the unfairness of having to stay home and eat liver for dinner with our uncle while waiting for news about my wounded twin. Mark had a concussion and had a short hospital stay and got lots of attention, while I felt like I got the worse end of the deal.

This was only one of Mark's many hospital stays during our childhood. Mark broke his arm sliding down a handrail. Mark had appendicitis. Mark stepped on a broken glass bottle of worms and got blood poisoning. Mark was taken into the city for a series of tests to see whether he had bone cancer (he didn't). We both played with BB guns recklessly, but only Mark got shot in the foot and then damaged by a botched surgery.

As our childhoods went on, we continued to take crazy risks. We both got hurt. We both got stitches so often we sometimes would have the doctors remove the stitches from the previous injury during the same visit new stitches were put in. But only Mark had to stay overnight at the hospital. I was always jealous of the extra attention this got him.

When we were about five, my parents bought a little vacation bungalow on the Jersey Shore, and some of my best memories from childhood are from that time.

At the shore, in the mornings, Mark and I had a kind of freedom my own children never had. We'd spend all day on the dock behind our bungalow, waiting to feel a crab nibble on the bait. We built rafts out of spare fence planks and set sail on Barnegat Bay. I remember falling off a dock before I knew how to swim and sinking into the dark and murky water of the lagoon. I didn't know what to do about it. I simply watched the bubbles of the last of my air rising. Then my father, who had seen my blond hair drifting just above the water, grabbed a handful and pulled me out.

When Mark and I were in second grade, our parents sold the place on the Jersey Shore so they could buy a house "up the hill." They wanted us to be able to go to a better public school. We moved onto a street lined with giant green oak trees, aptly named Greenwood Avenue. It's odd that once we moved, we hardly ever saw our family on Mitchell Street again. Except for his parents, my father was often not on speaking terms with various friends and family members.

We may have lived up the hill now, but we really still belonged down the hill. We stuck out among the wealthier families who lived nearby. Mark and I used to get into scrapes with neighbor kids—snowball fights, rock fights, apple fights with the crab apples that fell off the trees. We were like juvenile delinquents who never got arrested, probably because we were the children of a cop.

Mark and I both thought trying something hard was the only way to live. We threw ourselves off things, crawled under things, took dares from other boys, skated and slid and swam and capsized, sometimes tempting death. Mark and I climbed up drainpipes starting when we were six, waving back down at our parents from roofs two or three stories up. If we were doing something safe, something everyone already knew could be done, we thought we were wasting time.

I found it impossible to understand how my classmates could just sit still, breathing and blinking, for entire school days. How could they resist the urge to run outside, to take off exploring, to do something new, to take risks? What went through their heads? What could they learn in a classroom that could even come close to the feeling of flying down a hill out of control on a bike?

My brother and I used to spend one night a week with my father's parents, whom I loved, so our parents could go out. My grandmother, Helen, was so happy to see us every weekend and was always kind and loving. She let us watch all the TV we wanted and sang us to sleep. My grandfather had a great sense of humor, and he made a good life for himself and his family despite having only a sixth-grade education.

In the mornings, our grandparents always took us to the same diner for breakfast. After that we would spend hours visiting the flower gardens surrounding the historic mansions in northern New Jersey. That's how I started to love flowers and gardening, which would come back to me during my year in space, when I was tasked with bringing a crop of zinnias back from the brink of death. As much as I loved the breakfast and the flowers, my favorite part of these weekend visits was the routine—the way we did the same things in the same order. The calm and loving visits with my grandparents were like an oasis of safety in our lives. My father was an alcoholic, making life at home with our parents very chaotic.

Unfortunately, when my brother and I were maybe nine or ten, my parents decided we didn't need to be taken care of anymore when they went out. They'd come home in the middle of the night, drunk and loud. The sounds would first sneak into my dreams— the shouting and banging starting off low. But then it would gradually get louder, and Mark and I would eventually be lying awake in the dark, hearts pounding, listening to them fighting.

I've heard it said that the children of fighters grow up to become peacemakers. Maybe there's something to this, because my brother and I are two of the most stable, flexible, calm people I know.

My dad was good-looking and charming when he wasn't drinking, and to me he seemed just like a TV detective, a larger-than-life figure hunting down bad guys. I respected him, even idolized him in some ways, when I was young.

My parents bought a series of broken-down boats. We would take them out into the Atlantic Ocean, well past the horizon. We'd go out in any kind of weather, sometimes straight into a blinding fog with just a compass. We'd fish all day, and when it was time to come back in, we'd try to follow the charter fishing boats back into the inlet. If we lost them, we'd just head west until we saw land, then motor up or down the coast until we saw something we recognized. Often, our crappy engine would break down and we would drift until we could flag down another boat, since we didn't have a radio, to call the Coast Guard to tow us in. Sometimes we would even be taking on water, in danger of sinking. Each time, we'd get home, congratulate ourselves for surviving, and look forward to the next trip. It never occurred to us that we should stop taking these risks, because we always survived by our wits, always seemed to learn something from it. No wonder Mark and I loved taking chances.

When I was about eleven, my mother decided to become a cop. She'd done catering or babysitting to make extra money throughout my childhood. After that she'd become a secretary, which didn't pay well. Mom wanted a career and there weren't a lot of choices for women in the 1970s. Then the local police department offered women the chance to take the entrance exam. A lot of male police officers would have felt threatened by the thought of their wives trying to become officers as well. But not my father. To his credit, he helped her.

My mother had to study and pass a written test, which took time and effort. After she passed that, she had to take a tough physical fitness exam. She would have to meet all the same benchmarks as the men, and for a small woman, this was a big challenge. My father helped her set up an obstacle course in our backyard where she could practice every day. She ran around a set of cones carrying a toolbox filled with weights. She practiced dragging me a hundred feet across the backyard (in place of the dummy she would have to drag in the real test).

My mother practices dragging me like a victim to train for her police physical exam. August 1977.

My mother climbs over the practice wall my father built in our yard. August 1977.

The toughest part was the wall she would have to scale, seven feet, four inches tall. Knowing that, my father built a practice wall a bit higher than the real one. At first, Mom couldn't touch the top. It took her a long time before she was able to jump up and grab the top of the wall. Eventually she was able to pull herself up and get a leg over. After practicing every day, she was able to scale that wall on the first try every time. The day of the test, she actually scaled the wall better than most of the men. She became one of very few women to pass the test, and that made a big impression on Mark and me. Mom had decided on a goal that seemed almost impossible. And she reached that goal through personal determination and the help of the people around her.

My father holds the Bible as my mother gets sworn in as the first female officer in West Orange, New Jersey. August 1979.

I hadn't yet found a goal for myself that would give me that same kind of drive, but I had at least seen what that would look like.

2

EDUCATION IS VERY important—especially if you want to be an astronaut. I know that now, and I've worked hard at my studies to achieve my goals. But I owe all of my teachers a big apology because my memories of school are of being trapped in a classroom, bored out of my mind and always wondering what was going on outside. For my entire K–12 education, I basically ignored my teachers and daydreamed. I didn't know what I wanted to do, just that it would be exceptional. And I was pretty sure it had nothing to do with history, grammar, or algebra. I couldn't concentrate on anything. And in elementary school I was reading way behind grade level.

If I was growing up now, I probably would be diagnosed with ADHD. But back then, I was just considered a bad student. I learned to squeak by on whatever native intelligence I had, even though I never did any homework. One day in high school, our father sat us down and explained that college isn't the right choice for every person, and he could get us into a welders' union when we graduated. He believed a trade would be our best option for a career because we were such poor students. Mark realized right away that he wanted to do something different with his life, so he was motivated to improve his grades

from that day on. I don't even remember this conversation.
I was probably looking out the window at a squirrel.

The principal of our high school, Mr. Tarnoff, was the next
adult to try to convince me to put more effort into my schoolwork. He believed I had the potential to succeed if I could just
focus. I tried to explain to him how impossible it was for me to
pay attention in class.

Mr. Tarnoff, my high school principal, at one of my shuttle launches. He always
believed in me, even when I wasn't the best student. December 5, 2001.

After that conversation, I would avoid him whenever I saw him
in the hallways. I was surprised by how much it bothered me to
know I had let him down. Still, he never gave up on me. Years later,
he came to both of my space shuttle launches, and I think it meant
a lot to him to see that his faith in me had paid off.

I didn't find something I was good at that adults could approve
of until I got an after-school job in high school working as a volunteer emergency medical technician (EMT). Mark worked with the

local volunteer ambulance unit, too. When I took the EMT classes, I discovered that I had the patience to sit down and study. I was dealing with life-and-death situations in this job, and it was never boring. At night, I rode around the city in an ambulance, swooping in to help people in the worst moments of their lives. In the morning, I often drove home and went to sleep instead of going to school.

I had found something that was meaningful to me and that I was good at. So I decided to become a doctor—even though I graduated high school in the bottom half of my class. I knew I could be a good doctor—if I could just get through college, medical school, and the on-the-job training called residency.

Mark (left) and me (right) with our grandparents, dressed for our high school graduation. June 1983.

I was accepted to only one college, the University of Maryland, Baltimore County, so that was where I went. I started freshman year with great hope that I could turn things around and be a good student. I signed up for premed classes but was failing them by the end of my first semester.

Once again I realized that it was impossible for me to concentrate in class or study on my own. Soon I was struggling to think of a reason to go to class, knowing I wouldn't absorb any of the professor's lecture. Often, I just didn't go. How was I even going to graduate college with the grades I was getting? Medical school seemed like an impossible dream.

Everything changed one day when I walked into the campus bookstore to buy snacks and a book display caught my eye. The letters on the book's cover seemed to streak into the future. I wasn't much of a reader—whenever I was assigned to read a book for school, I would barely flip through it, hopelessly bored. Sometimes I'd read enough to pass a test on the book, sometimes not. I had not read many books by choice in my entire life—but this book, *The Right Stuff* by Tom Wolfe, somehow called to me from the bookshelf.

I picked up a copy, and the first sentences I read instantly dropped me into a smoky field at the naval air station in Jacksonville, Florida, where a young test pilot had just been killed after he crashed his airplane into a tree. The scene captured my attention like nothing else I had ever read.

I bought the book and lay down on my unmade dorm room bed, reading for the rest of the day, heart pounding. Tom Wolfe's looping sentences filled my head. I was captivated by the description of the Navy test pilots catapulting off aircraft carriers, testing unstable airplanes, and generally moving through the world like young hotshots.

According to Wolfe, a pilot had to be able to take off "in a hurtling piece of machinery and put his hide on the line" to test the limits of his aircraft. He then had to have "the moxie, the reflexes, the experience, the coolness, to pull it back in the last yawning moment—and then to go up again *the next day*, and the next day, and every next day." The pilots took these risks, not for their own glory, but "in a cause that means something to thousands, to a people, a nation, to humanity, to God."

The Mercury 7, NASA's first astronauts, were all top military pilots—and my inspiration. From left to right: Scott Carpenter, Gordon "Gordo" Cooper Jr., John Glenn Jr., Virgil "Gus" Grissom, Walter "Wally" Schirra Jr., Alan Shepard Jr., and Donald "Deke" Slayton. January 20, 1961.

This wasn't just an exciting adventure story to me. These young men, flying jets in the Navy, did a real job that existed in the real world. These were hard jobs to get, I understood, but some people did get them. It could be done. I wanted to be like the guys in this book, guys who could land a jet on an aircraft carrier at night and then walk away with a swagger. I wanted to be a naval aviator.

Here, in a book, I found something I'd thought I would never find: my life's purpose. I closed the book late that night a different person. I was still an eighteen-year-old with terrible grades who knew nothing about airplanes. But *The Right Stuff* had given me the outline of a life plan.

For the rest of that fall of 1982, I walked around campus with a new outlook on life. Before, I had always wondered where everyone got the motivation to get out of bed early to make it to class. Now I knew why: they each had some kind of goal. Now I'd found mine, too, and it was a great feeling. Not only was I going to become a Navy pilot, I might even become an astronaut. And I was ready to get started right now.

If the Mercury 7 could go from pilots to astronauts, maybe I could, too. Front row, left to right: Walter "Wally" Schirra Jr., Donald "Deke" Slayton, John Glenn Jr., Scott Carpenter. Back row, left to right: Alan Shepard Jr., Virgil "Gus" Grissom, and Gordon "Gordo" Cooper Jr. April 9, 1959.

I just had one problem: the path to becoming a naval aviator is an extremely competitive one, and I was still a poor student with terrible grades. I needed to become a commissioned officer in the Navy, but my path was blocked by much better students who had already been nominated to the U.S. Naval Academy by their congressman or senator. They had aced their SATs. Because I'd daydreamed my way through high school, I didn't have the basic knowledge even to begin the kinds of courses I'd have to take: calculus, physics, engineering. Beyond that, I knew that even if I started at the easiest classes, I still probably wouldn't be able to keep up. I may have the will, but I lacked the skills I needed to learn.

Everywhere I looked, I saw students who could listen to the teacher in class and ask smart questions and write down notes. They turned in homework assignments on time, correctly done. They did something they called "studying." They were then able to do well on exams. I had no idea how to do any of this. If you've never felt this way, it's hard to tell you how awful it is.

By now, my brother was a freshman at the U.S. Merchant Marine Academy, in Kings Point, New York. Given my new goals, this seemed like a good place to start for me, too, because Kings Point offered a path to a commission in the Navy. It would also give me the structure of a military environment, which I felt I needed. Best of all, Mark could help me get used to the new school and new routines. Unfortunately, the dean of admissions at Kings Point didn't think I had the right stuff to attend their school.

Kings Point had seemed to be my only possibility: If I couldn't get accepted there, I believed I would meet rejection anywhere else I tried. I would be years behind all the people I'll be competing with, and maybe the Navy wouldn't want me anymore.

Everything else I'd done in my life up to this point, like working as an EMT, had played to my strengths. This new goal was going to expose every weakness I had.

When I started my second semester at the University of Maryland, I took more difficult classes and worked hard for the first time in my life. I remember walking into my math class on the first day thinking, *This is it. If I can't show what I'm capable of in this class, I'm not going to get the chance to do much more.*

After class, I sat down to do the homework, feeling the pressure of everything I had now decided to do. I had to force myself to stay in my chair. I kept thinking of something else I needed to do in another room. I needed to sharpen my pencil. I needed a glass of water. I stayed in the chair anyway. I forced myself to read through the chapter over and over. I forced myself to work through the homework problems, and while I was pretty sure I had gotten the right answers to the easier ones, the harder questions were still challenging. It was late at night by the time I was done. I tried to focus on the fact that I had set myself a goal—to read this chapter, to do the math problems—and I had done that. I turned out the light feeling like I might finally be able to turn things around.

A few weeks later, I realized that it was getting a *little* easier to do my homework. It was still a mighty struggle to stay in the chair, and I only got a B− in the class. Still, that B− was one of the major achievements of my life so far.

This gave me hope that maybe another school would accept me. So I applied to transfer to two schools: Rutgers University and the State University of New York Maritime College. Both were close by, and both offered me the possibility of becoming an officer in the Navy.

SUNY Maritime is a small military-oriented school in the Bronx, established to train ships' officers in the maritime industry. It was the first maritime college in the country, built on Fort Schuyler (named for General Philip Schuyler, Alexander Hamilton's father-in-law). The fort was designed to defend Manhattan from naval attack in the aftermath of the War of 1812. When the school made me an offer of admission, I immediately accepted. I had just barely made the cutoff.

3

I **KNEW WHEN** I started Maritime in the summer of 1983 it would be like joining the military. I knew the year would begin with a two-week introductory program called indoctrination, but I had only a hazy idea based on movies of what this would be like: getting my head shaved, having upperclassmen shout in my face, forced marches, having to clean things like shoes and belt buckles over and over. As it turned out, all of these ideas were entirely true.

The SUNY Maritime campus was surprisingly beautiful, on a spit of land between the Long Island Sound and the East River, under the Throgs Neck Bridge.

The military discipline came pretty easily for me. It was almost a relief to be told what to do and how to do it. Many of my classmates tried to cut corners, and whined and complained. But I had started to figure out that I needed a clear challenge in order to apply myself. Schoolwork was still hard for me, but following directions gave me stability. I embraced it.

At the end of the indoctrination, we had a ceremony to mark the achievement. My parents and my paternal grandparents came, and as we marched by in formation, I saw all of them in the stands looking proudly at me. I was surprised by how much it meant to me to have them there, to have given them something to be proud of. But I was also aware of how far I still had to go.

I started the regular school year as a freshman. Because the program here was so different, I had to do my first year of college all over again. I was taking six classes: calculus, physics, electrical engineering, seamanship, and military history. The work was challenging even for my classmates who had excelled in high school, and I felt good about the fact that I was keeping my head above water.

My freshman school picture at Maritime College, New York. Fall 1983.

When Labor Day weekend approached, I got a call from one of my high school buddies inviting me to a party at Rutgers. I said I'd be there.

I called my brother. "Let's go down to Rutgers and hang out," I said.

"I can't," Mark said right away. "I have a test coming up."

I spent a few minutes trying to talk him into it before he interrupted.

"Don't you have some sort of test coming up, too? You've been in classes for a few weeks now."

"Yeah," I admitted. "My first calculus exam is at the end of next week. But I'll study for it after I get back. I'll have Tuesday, Wednesday, Thursday. . . ."

"Are you out of your mind?" Mark asked. "You need to spend this entire weekend at your desk, doing every problem in every chapter this exam is going to cover."

"Seriously?" I asked. "The entire long weekend?" This sounded insane to me.

I didn't appreciate being yelled at by my twin brother. It was tempting to tell myself he was just being a jerk and that I should ignore him. I came so close to deciding not to listen; the memory still unsettles me, like a memory of teetering on the edge of a cliff. As much as I wanted to go to the party, I knew somewhere in my mind that he was right. And I needed him to hit me over the head with this so I could really *hear* him. Mark had decided to pull himself together long before I did and had succeeded. I'd never asked him how he'd done it, but now he was trying to offer me the lesson of his experience. I reluctantly decided to listen.

I stayed in all weekend—hard as it was for me—and worked

every problem in every chapter, just as he had suggested, until I could do them all. When I took the exam that Friday, I felt for the first time in my life as though I understood every question and thought I had answered them more or less correctly. It was a strange feeling. When we got our exams back the next week, there was a circled red 100 at the top of mine. I had earned a perfect score on a test for the first time in my life, and on a math test to boot. This was how people got good grades. It was like a door had opened.

From that point on, I enjoyed the challenge of school. I worked hard and enjoyed seeing it pay off. It almost became a game I played with myself: let's see how well I can do at this. In a strange way, it was easier for me to get an A+ than it would have been to get a B. I needed to be all in, or I would mess up. I decided to try to know *everything*. Then I would always get an A.

That phone call with Mark changed my life almost as much as reading *The Right Stuff*. The book had given me a vision of who I wanted to be; my brother's advice showed me how to get there.

Soon after classes got started, I joined the Navy ROTC, which stands for Reserve Officers Training Corp—my path into the Navy. So I trained with the other cadets, doing military drills and taking classes on leadership, weapons systems, and military etiquette. After my first semester with nearly straight A's, I was offered a Navy ROTC scholarship. I was pleased to be that much closer to my ultimate goals, and of course my parents were pleased that the rest of my tuition would be paid for.

After the school year, we spent a few weeks preparing our training ship for our first cruise—to Europe. In the summer of 1984, the *Empire State V* was crewed by the cadets, and we each had assigned tasks on the ship throughout the cruise.

The living conditions aboard the ship were dark and dingy. When I headed up to the mess deck, our floating cafeteria, for meals, I often came across people throwing up into the large trash cans that lined the room. At night, people moaned in their bunks from nausea. I seemed to be immune to seasickness, and I hoped the same would be true for flight and eventually into space.

We worked on a three-day cycle: maintain the ship one day, stand watch one day, and attend classes one day. The best watch to draw was helm, as we would actually get to have a hand on the wheel steering the ship. Bow watch meant just looking out over the water trying to identify other ships. Stern watch, on the back of the ship, meant looking out for someone falling overboard, which no one ever did.

We came back to Maritime stronger and smarter than when we'd left. We'd learned to work together, responded to the unexpected, and survived. I stepped off the *Empire State* V a different person than when I'd stepped on.

As soon as I finished that first cruise, I got on a plane to Long Beach, California, to do freshman ROTC training on a Navy ship cruising to Hawaii. I was with midshipmen from other colleges, including the Naval Academy, who were doing all of this for the first time. Though I was only a few months ahead of them in sailing experience, it seemed like much more.

This was my first real exposure to the Navy. Midshipmen were expected to do the work of enlisted sailors, so when they became officers leading enlisted sailors, they would know what their responsibilities were like. I lived in crowded bunks again, with about twenty guys stacked three bunks high. It was good practice for living in small spaces in the future.

At the start of my junior year, I had been appointed the chief indoctrination officer for the class, in charge of supervising all those running the grueling period of drills and training the incoming freshmen. It was a demanding job but a huge honor—it meant that my superiors saw leadership potential in me. I was determined to prove them right.

I had 250 new MUGs (Midshipmen Under Guidance) to train. I was responsible for teaching them the traditions and expectations of Maritime, as well as helping them adjust to life away from home. As the final authority on discipline, I had decided that I wanted to be the kind of leader who was firm but fair.

I once received an anonymous note from a MUG warning me not to get too close to the ship's railing at night on our next cruise—a threat to push me overboard. This was an early lesson that a leader can't always please everyone. I can understand why this MUG and the others I dealt with found the rules so difficult. But I had come to believe that shining shoes and polishing belt buckles helped us to learn the attention to detail required to safely and effectively operate at sea.

Each summer, we took the *Empire State* V to new ports, and immediately after I returned from each of those cruises, I would then leave for my Navy cruise.

In my senior year, I was named the battalion commander of my Navy ROTC unit, another leadership role. By that time, I was taking harder classes than ever, mostly electrical engineering. I now knew how to study and took pride in it. In fact, I actually enjoyed it, something I never thought would happen.

It was still my goal to become a Navy pilot, specifically to fly jets off an aircraft carrier. In college, I had been doing whatever I could to improve my chances, including caring for my vision. A lot of my friends who hoped to become pilots became a bit obsessed. We all knew some poor guy who had worked all his life toward becoming a Navy pilot only to be rejected for having vision slightly less than 20/20. I made sure to always have a bright light to read by.

Early in my senior year, I took a standardized test called the Aviation Qualification Test/Flight Aptitude Rating. The test measures the way a student thinks, like an IQ test, and the way a student sees, using visual puzzles.

I knew how important this test would be to my future, so I worked hard to prepare for it. The day of the exam, I left the classroom feeling like I had done as well as I possibly could. I wouldn't know for weeks what my results were. After that it would take months before I would learn which part of the Navy I would be assigned to, or if I would be chosen for aviation, much less that I would go on to fly jets.

One cold day in January, my roommate George Lang and I were sitting in our room just after lunch, watching *Star Trek* on our tiny color TV. A news anchor broke into the show to report that the space shuttle *Challenger* had exploded seventy-three seconds after launch. We watched the shuttle blow up on the screen over and over, killing all seven astronauts on board.

It took weeks after the accident before anyone had a good

idea about what caused this tragedy. Eventually it was confirmed that the unusually cold weather in Florida had caused a rubber O-ring in one of the solid rocket boosters to fail.

The *Challenger* explosion was one of NASA's worst tragedies, killing all seven crew members—including America's first teacher in space, Christa McAuliffe—and the rest of the crew: Greg Jarvis, Ron McNair, Ellison Onizuka, Judith Resnick, Dick Scobee, and Mike Smith. January 28, 1986.

"You still want to do it?" George asked me after a few hours of watching the tragedy nonstop.

"What do you mean?" I asked.

"The shuttle," George said. "You still want to fly on it?"

"Absolutely," I said, and I meant it. My determination to fly difficult aircraft had only grown stronger, and the space shuttle was the most difficult aircraft (and spacecraft) of all. The *Challenger* disaster had made clear that spaceflight was dangerous, but I already knew that. I felt confident that NASA would find the cause of the explosion, that it would be fixed, and that the space shuttle would be a better vehicle as a result. It sounds strange, but seeing the risk involved only made flying in space seem more appealing.

When I graduated from Maritime, I was a completely different person from the confused kid who had entered four years earlier. I was so grateful to the school for everything it had done for me.

I earned a high score on the aviation qualification test, and soon after graduation I was assigned to flight school in Pensacola, Florida. I packed all my belongings into my old white BMW and drove south that summer of 1987.

My graduation photo from Maritime College, in the shadow of the Throgs Neck Bridge, New York. May 9, 1987.

4

PENSACOLA IS ON Florida's panhandle. It's a typical military town set against a background of beautiful beaches. Pensacola was the top of the world for a young officer like me. I drove around feeling like a rock star.

Flight school started with several weeks of tough physical, swim, and survival training. There was a cross-country course we had to navigate in a certain amount of time, an obstacle course with hurdles to jump over, barriers to shimmy under, sand to crawl through, a wall to climb. The film *An Officer and a Gentleman* gives a pretty accurate picture of what aviation indoctrination training was like, and just as in the film, we student naval aviators had to conquer the Dilbert Dunker a few weeks in.

The dunker is designed to give a pilot the unpleasant experience of a water landing, known as ditching, in an airplane—basically crashing into the water. Dressed in full flight gear and helmet, each pilot was strapped into a mock-up cockpit that was then sent down a steep rail into the deep end of a swimming pool. During this test, we'd hit the water hard enough to knock the wind out of some of us. Once submerged, we'd have only a few seconds to get our bearings before the cockpit turned upside down. Then we'd have to detach the comm wire, release the restraints while hanging upside down, find our way out of the cockpit, and then dive deeper in order to escape the fuel that might be burning on the ocean surface in a real ditching. A few people who went through this before me couldn't find their way out and had to be pulled out of the cockpit by rescue divers. Luckily, when I hit the water, I managed to find my way out on the first try.

We also had to go through a similar dunker that simulated a helicopter crash in water. People have drowned in the helo dunker, and I heard that some even went into cardiac arrest. I couldn't have been happier when I passed the test.

The swim requirements were even harder. We had to be able to swim a mile and tread water for fifteen minutes, in full flight suit and boots. I got through the mile swim easily, but I found treading water so hard! Other guys seemed to float naturally; I seemed to sink like a brick. I practiced and practiced and was finally able to pass the requirement, though just barely.

I also learned various survival techniques in water, like making a flotation device out of my pants, and drownproofing—floating facedown in the water and bringing my mouth to the surface only when I needed to take a breath.

One day we were taken in groups to experience the altitude chamber, a sealed room in which the air pressure is slowly lowered to give us a chance to see how low oxygen levels make us feel. Symptoms could include tingling in the hands and feet, nails and lips turning blue, trouble speaking clearly, and confusion. After a number of sessions in the chamber, I tried to push my limits to see how bad my symptoms could get and how I could control them. At first I started to feel a bit drunk and stupid. That feeling turned quickly into extreme happiness. Happiness became confusion, followed closely by tunnel vision, and the next thing I knew, the person watching my safety was putting my oxygen mask back on for me. I wasn't able to do it myself. The lesson I learned in the low-pressure chamber was that you can push yourself past your limits very quickly.

During flight school. A pilot in training escapes underwater from the Dilbert Dunker.

We also needed to do survival training in case our plane crashed on land and we were unable to be rescued for a time. We were dropped off in the woods for days to learn to build shelters, make signal fires, navigate the terrain, and feed ourselves on only what we could hunt or forage. We couldn't find anything to eat except for a rattlesnake we killed with a big stick.

Aviation school also required a great deal of studying. Most of the material was new to me, but it wasn't too different from what I had studied in college. I knew I could excel if I worked hard, so I did. The better I did at every part of our training, the better my chances would be of getting assigned to jets.

After we got through classroom and physical training successfully, which took about six weeks, it was finally time to learn to fly airplanes. We started off flying the T-34C Turbo Mentor, a propeller-driven trainer. The flight manuals we had to study were packed with charts and graphs and filled with unfamiliar terms and abbreviations. The material was hard to get through, but we had to master it before we could fly.

When I was declared ready, the first phase of my actual flight training began. In the briefing room, I met Lieutenant Lex Lauletta, my on-wing instructor, a tall blond guy who greeted me with a friendly smile. That set me at ease, since some of the instructors were said to give a hard time to guys like me who were dead set on flying jets. I would do most of my initial flights with him, and he kept me from killing myself while he taught me. He would also be grading me, which would help determine whether I would get to fly jets, helicopters, larger fixed-wing airplanes—or nothing at all.

During our initial meeting, I tried on my own "green bag," or flight suit, for the first time. For me, this was like getting assigned a uniform you get to wear for the rest of your flying life that instantly lets people know you're a hotshot Navy pilot.

Out on the airfield, I saw hundreds of T-34s lined up, one after another. Lieutenant Lauletta figured out which one was ours. As we walked toward it, he gave me my first lesson about how not to get killed: never walk near a propeller, even if you know it isn't turning. I was excited and nervous when we walked out to the airplane for the first time. I had worked so hard to get to this point, but I still had no idea if I could actually fly a plane. Some people can't, no matter how hard they try, and you can't know that until you're up in the air.

A tarmac full of T-34C Turbo Mentors, our training plane of choice.

The first moment I settled down into the seat was surreal. On the one hand, it was the end of a long hard journey that started when I first cracked the cover of *The Right Stuff*. There had been many moments when it seemed that I wasn't going to make it. Now I could say I had—I was a student naval aviator. On the other hand, this was going to be the start of a whole new set of challenges.

Lauletta helped me get strapped in properly; then we both closed the canopies over our cockpits. I'd studied diagrams of the controls of the T-34 in the flight manual as if my life depended on understanding them (because it would). I'd learned them and practiced using them in the simulator. Now they seemed to have multiplied into a field of thousands of knobs, switches, gauges, and handles. I had to tell myself to get on with it, that I was ready to do this. It was time to start the plane.

Under Lauletta's instruction, I applied power and started moving forward. Taxiing was more difficult than I had anticipated. I felt like I was learning to ride a bike, trying to keep my balance with someone watching over my shoulder the whole time, grading me. I was already struggling.

A pilot must also learn to use the radio, which is harder than you would think. Talking and doing anything else at the same time can be challenging, as it requires using two different parts of the brain. And of course I wanted a cool Navy radio voice. When Lauletta cued me, I spoke into the radio and said, "Whiting tower, Red Knight Four Seven One ready for takeoff."

Somehow this did not sound nearly cool enough to me. I felt like a little kid playing make-believe. But the tower responded as if my call had been legitimate. "Roger, Red Knight Four Seven One, taxi to position and hold." This meant we could head out onto the runway but weren't cleared for takeoff yet. Eventually the tower came back: "Red Knight Four Seven One, you are cleared for takeoff."

I accelerated down the runway, trying my hardest to keep the airplane pointed in the right direction. Once I was going faster, it was a bit easier to control the plane's direction, and with

Lauletta's instruction I slowly pulled back on the stick to make the nose come off the ground. The runway, buildings, and trees tilted back and fell away as we pointed up into the sky. We bounced up and down as I struggled to find the proper attitude, the position of the plane relative to the ground, but we were airborne. In that moment, I was elated. I was flying a plane—however poorly.

Once I was settled into the flight, I had to concentrate on maintaining altitude. Although we were going only 120 miles per hour, I lifted and dropped us wildly, struggling to keep the airplane within five hundred feet of our intended altitude. Years later I would fly the F-14 Tomcat at more than twice the speed of sound and control the space shuttle in the atmosphere and in space many times faster, but nothing ever felt as hard to control as that training airplane on that first flight. It seemed to resist my efforts at every turn.

After about forty-five minutes of demonstrating how bad I was at this, I was relieved when Lauletta directed me toward an outlying airfield so we could practice touch-and-go landings. He demonstrated the first one, carefully describing everything he was doing. He made it look easy. Now it was my turn.

Despite the airplane being small and the runway large, I had a surprisingly hard time landing. Eventually I managed to smack the wheels down onto the runway without killing us. Then I immediately took off to do it one more time, then another, then another. And still I didn't feel I was getting any better.

Clearly this was going to take some time to learn, and nothing about it was going to come easily. Still, Lauletta said I had done pretty well for my first day.

After twelve flights with an instructor over a period of several months, I was declared "safe for solo."

Me at Naval Air Station Whiting Field, Florida, as a young Naval officer prior to a flight in a T-34C training aircraft. Circa fall 1987.

The first time a pilot flies solo is a big day. I climbed into the airplane feeling nervous. The weather was perfect, though, with clear skies and low winds. After a good takeoff and flying for about an hour and a half without crashing into anything, it was time to land. I was so focused on all the things I needed to do to land the airplane that I released the landing gear too early. I was still going so fast the landing gear could be damaged or might even break off, which would make it impossible to land. I knew I had messed this up the second I did it, but there was no way to undo it. I had to fess up.

I called down to the tower. "Tower, Red Knight Eight Three Two."

"Go ahead, Red Knight Eight Three Two."

"I lowered the landing gear too fast, but all the gear are showing down and locked." I cringed as I waited for the response to come back.

"Okay, circle overhead at fifteen hundred feet until we figure out what we want to do. How much fuel do you have?"

I reported the fuel level, feeling relieved that the controller didn't seem very alarmed. The decision was made to have me fly by the tower so the controller could look at my landing gear. After my flyby, he could see that everything was fine, and I was allowed to land.

It's not unusual for a student pilot to make this kind of error on a first flight, and I knew I could recover from it. Still, I was disappointed. I'd wanted to absolutely nail everything the first time I soloed.

There is a saying in the Navy about mistakes: "There are those who have and those who will." It's easy to look at someone else's screwup and say, "I never would have done that." But you could have, and you still may. Remembering this can guard against the kind of cockiness that gets pilots killed. So my mistake with the landing gear was a good early lesson.

Once I had soloed a few times, I started learning aerobatics—loops, rolls, and other more complex maneuvers. I went out with an instructor again, listening while he explained what he was about to demonstrate. When it was my turn to take the controls, I found I had a real knack for flying around the big, puffy clouds and rolling the airplane upside down and all around whenever I wanted. And I enjoyed this part of the training—the sense of freedom it gave me—more than anything else. Even better, I never felt like I was disoriented or sick, which happened to some of the other newbie pilots. It felt great to find an aspect of flying I was good at! Only a small percentage of those who start flight school wind up being assigned to a jet squadron. I had done everything I could to earn a place among them.

The day our next assignments in flight school were announced, a secretary tacked a simple sheet of paper to the bulletin board in the hall. We all crowded around. The list had ten names on it in alphabetical order, and next to each name was an assignment. Next to KELLY, SCOTT I found the words BEEVILLE NAVAL AIR STATION. I had done it! I was one of only two guys in my group to make it to jets. I felt for my friends who didn't, but I was thrilled to know that my dream was still alive.

5

In the spring of 1988, I moved to Beeville, Texas, a small dusty town of blowing tumbleweeds halfway between Corpus Christi and San Antonio. Beeville is one of a few centers of the universe for young Navy pilots who want to fly jets, and I was thrilled to be there.

The first time I put on a G suit and climbed into the cockpit, I felt like I had arrived in the big leagues. G suits are needed to keep pilots from passing out from the effects of fast acceleration, known as g's, caused by pulling back on the control stick. The fast acceleration makes pilots feel much heavier and causes the blood to drain from their heads. I began flying the T-2 Buckeye, a twin-engine jet. The T-2 is a relatively easy jet to operate, which is why we trained on it first, but it's still a jet nonetheless and danger-ous to fly. A jet has a lot more power than a propeller-driven air-plane. It can go faster, quicker, and responds to the pilot's slightest touch—all of which make it much easier to "get behind" the air-plane (when it feels like the airplane is in control rather than the pilot) and get into trouble. I had a lot to learn.

Wearing an oxygen mask and G suit and flying while strapped into an ejection seat made me more aware of the potential dan-ger that came with flying a jet. It was more intimidating than I had anticipated.

Me in the cockpit of the F-14 Tomcat wearing an oxygen mask and helmet. Circa 1991.

After I had flown that airplane for about a hundred hours, it was time to try landing on an aircraft carrier—a Navy ship with a flight deck to launch and land airplanes. Because an aircraft carrier's flight deck is so short, it has special equipment to help the aircraft take off and land. Catapults help planes to launch quickly, and arresting cables help them stop before they fly off the end of the deck. The landings are difficult and dangerous, even under the best circumstances.

This is the point in training when a lot of pilots wash out. I'd known this from the start, thanks to *The Right Stuff*. Carrier qualifications would be flown out of Pensacola. I flew there a day early and met my brother and some of his squadron mates. Mark was a year ahead of me, since I had to repeat my freshman year of college. He had gone to Corpus Christi for flight training and had just qualified for both day and night landings on the carrier. Mark would soon be moving on to his fleet squadron, stationed in Japan.

The flight deck of an aircraft carrier is an incredibly dangerous place. It's not uncommon for people to be killed or seriously injured there, despite the high level of training. People have died walking into spinning propeller blades, getting sucked down a jet intake, or being blown over the side by a plane's exhaust. Many of the personnel are teenagers who face a lot of responsibility and risk. To avoid accidents, everyone must know exactly what his or her job is and perform it well. Mine was to land the plane.

The day of my qualifying test, the weather was not great. As I flew closer to the ship, I looked down at the USS *Lexington* in the water and couldn't believe I was going to have to land my jet on that tiny dot. When you land an airplane at an airport, the runway is generally at least 7,000 feet long and 150 feet wide. The runway on an aircraft carrier is less than 1,000 feet in length and half as narrow. More important, though, an airport runway doesn't move, while a ship's runway moves up and down and side to side along with the ocean's swells. At the same time, the ship is also moving forward in the water, so the landing area is constantly moving away from the jet trying to land on it.

The sight of the ship scared me a little because my landings still weren't very precise. As I approached for my first landing, I hit one end of the deck, then punched to full power to head back off into the air at the other end of the ship. I needed to do six touch-and-goes—landing and taking off again immediately—to get the feel of landing on the deck. After that, I could touch down and extend my plane's tailhook to grab the arresting cable on the flight deck that would bring my jet to a quick stop. This is called an arrested landing. What makes an arrested landing even more dangerous is that a pilot has to accurately hit the deck, then quickly rev the engine up to full power in case the tailhook misses the arresting cable. This enables the jet to leap back into the sky instead of sliding off the front end of the deck into the water.

My first touch-and-go attempt hadn't gone badly, and now I was slightly more confident. I'd have to make four arrested landings in order to pass my qualifying test, and I hoped to make them all that day.

I got through all my touch-and-goes with no problem. But when I put the hook down while approaching the ship, the danger of the situation became more real to me. I felt my heart pounding—not a good thing. I approached, touched down, and went to full power in case the hook missed the wires. The feeling when my hook caught the wires and confirmed that I had done everything right would have been fantastic—if I hadn't forgotten to lock my harness properly. As the arresting cable brought my plane to an instant stop, I was thrown forward and smashed into the instrument panel. I felt like I'd been in a car crash as I landed, making my first heart-stopping carrier landing even more terrifying. I was feeling dazed. I was now supposed to reduce the power once I came to a stop, but I was having trouble doing it quickly. One of the aircraft handlers ran out in front of the jet, wildly giving me the "power back" signal. With the handler's help, I was able to recover.

I did a second arrested landing, then another one. One more and I would have done all of the required four landings. Then it started getting dark, and we were all sent back to the airfield. I expected to go out the next day and do the last required landing for my qualification. But when I saw the next day's flight schedule and I wasn't on it, I assumed I had been disqualified for some reason. I was upset for a few hours, thinking that I had failed. I was surprised to learn that I had done well enough on the three landings I completed to be qualified without doing a fourth. I was officially a carrier aviator, also called a tailhooker.

Once I qualified in the T-2, I started flying the A-4 Skyhawk, an attack jet from the Vietnam era that let us learn more of the skills we would need for flying in combat: dropping bombs, flying at low altitude in order to avoid being seen on radar, and air combat maneuvering (ACM), also known as dogfighting. We were expected to learn quickly and move on to the next challenge. I wasn't especially gifted at dropping bombs, and nothing I tried to improve my accuracy seemed to work. I got used to taking ribbing from my classmates about it.

I was much more skilled at dogfighting. A lot of people tend to fly a plane in two dimensions (forward and back, side to side) as if driving a car. But for some reason, thinking in three dimensions (adding up and down), as you have to when dogfighting, came naturally to me. That gave me an advantage.

A common exercise we practiced was to start out flying side by side in a group. Then, at a point called the merge, we would turn and fly toward one another, trying to gain a better position. The fight started just as you passed another plane side by side, wing tip to wing tip. It was this exercise that taught me the truth of the naval aviator motto: "If you're not cheating, you're not trying hard enough." I learned that if I showed up at the merge with more air speed than I was supposed to have, I had a slight advantage.

Remember, we were being trained to fight a war, with our lives and the fate of our country on the line. So we'd need to do whatever we could to win. Off the battlefield, however, honor and honesty were valued above all else.

Dogfighting was one of my favorite phases of training, not only because I did well at it, but because it was fun. I experienced a freedom and creativity in air-to-air "combat" that I hadn't found anywhere else.

My training in Beeville took about a year. I felt great pride the day I got my wings. My parents came for the occasion (my brother was unable to attend because of his own Navy duties). We lined up in our white dress uniforms for the ceremonial pinning on of our wings. My mother pinned my wings on me, her face glowing with pride. I remembered the day she had graduated from the police academy, when I got to see her lined up with her classmates in uniform, and the impression that sight had made on me. Now things had come full circle.

I was assigned to Fighter Squadron 101, the Grim Reapers, and moved to Naval Air Station Oceana, in Virginia Beach, Virginia, for initial training on the F-14. My roommate and I drove overnight and I started my training almost the minute I got there. Just as I had done with other aircraft, I progressed quickly. This was where I began to feel like a true fighter pilot and learned basic air combat maneuvers.

My first two flights were with an experienced pilot in the back seat. After that, I flew only with an instructor RIO (Radar Intercept Officer, like Goose in the movie *Top Gun*).

We quickly advanced to learning to fly the airplane in combat, including shooting the gun. These exercises were done using real bullets, which seems like a terrible idea, though I never saw anyone get shot by accident. Each of us had bullets painted with a different color so the instructors would be able to tell who had hit the target how many times. Just as with bombing, I wasn't particularly good at this, but I always enjoyed competing.

Every time I learned to fly a new jet, I had to qualify to land it on an aircraft carrier. The night before I tried to land the F-14 for the first time on the carrier ship USS *Enterprise* off the coast of Virginia, I lay awake in bed for a long time. Our instructor had told us, "You won't be able to sleep, so just try to lie still and think about nothing so you get some rest." This turned out to be good advice and has served me well many times in the years since.

Arrested landings and catapult launches on an aircraft carrier are dangerous for both the pilot and the ship's crew. Here, I'm getting ready to launch from the USS *Enterprise*. Circa 1990.

My first arrested landing was a complete disaster. I landed so low that my tailhook hit the back of the ship. That's called a hook slap, and it's not good. Basically, if I'd been any lower I would have crashed, and that would have killed me and my RIO. While none of my other approaches were as bad as that hook slap, I didn't get much better. After a while, the instructors had seen enough and sent me home. I had disqualified.

I landed back at Naval Air Station Oceana with a weird feeling of disbelief. After my RIO and I jumped out of the plane, he looked at me with concern. I must have appeared as bewildered as I felt.

"Hey, you'll figure it out," he told me with an awkward pat on the shoulder. "Don't worry about it. Shake it off."

I could only mutter in response. There had been so much riding on this, and I had failed. I didn't understand what I was doing wrong, so I didn't know how I could improve if I got another chance. And it was possible I wouldn't get one.

In the end, they gave me a second chance. But I had to start all over in the carrier qualification phase, where I was paired up with a different RIO, Lieutenant Lang, who had a good reputation for helping pilots like me who were having trouble behind the boat.

"You know, you can fly the airplane okay, but you're not *flying* it all the time," he told me. I had been trained to stay within a two-hundred-foot range, so I didn't worry if my altitude varied within ten or twenty or fifty feet. But Lang pointed out that this lack of precision was my problem. And fixing it would take a lot of my attention. He was right, and I worked hard for the next few weeks to correct this. My flying got better, and I've been able to apply what I learned from him to a lot of other areas of life as well.

If we aren't always trying to make things at least a little bit better, they're going to get worse.

I did well enough flying during the day to have a chance to make my second attempt to qualify at night. It was an exceptionally dark night, black with no moonlight. As I got within a couple of miles I started peeking out from the cockpit to see whether I could spot the ship. It was disorienting to see the faint lights of the carrier in an ocean of black, like a tiny toy ship. At three-quarters of a mile, the air traffic controller told me to "call the ball," to start flying by sight (rather than using the aircraft's instruments). My first thought was, *Uh-oh,* but I flew as Lang had trained me to, making small corrections to line up with the ship. The glow of the flight deck became brighter until it was a big yellow haze. The next thing I knew, I felt the tug of the arresting cable. I had landed safely and successfully.

The day you qualify to land on an aircraft carrier is a big deal, and when you do it at night, it's an even bigger one. It was our squadron's tradition to celebrate with a party. And this party was at my house.

My roommate's girlfriend brought a friend to the party—Leslie Yandell. I remember seeing Leslie sitting on my couch talking with her friends. She was cute, with a bright smile and curly blond hair. I decided to talk to her for a bit and found out that she had grown up in Georgia but lived nearby. She was easy to talk with, and I liked her laugh, so I asked her out for the next weekend. She said yes.

Leslie and I dated regularly for most of that year. I enjoyed having Sunday dinners with her family. It seemed like a logical next step to propose. I asked Leslie to marry me while sitting on a park bench on the edge of the Chesapeake Bay, and she said yes. My brother had already been married for several years, and that added to the feeling that I should be ready for this stage of my life.

In September 1990, I was assigned to a real fighter squadron, VF-143, nicknamed the World Famous Pukin' Dogs. Being in an F-14 squadron in the 1990s was like a cross between playing a professional sport and being in a rock-and-roll band. The movie *Top Gun* didn't quite capture the arrogance and bravado of the pilots. I felt like I was living my dream. In September 1991, the squadron headed to the Red Sea, the Persian Gulf, and the fjords of Norway on the USS *Dwight D. Eisenhower*, nicknamed the *Ike*. Since the first Gulf War had ended earlier that year, most of my six-month deployment would be spent flying the F-14 nearly every other day to safeguard the air above the *Ike* from any threats—while also fitting in some training flights as well.

One black night only a few weeks into the cruise, my RIO Ward Carroll (whom we called Mooch) and I took up our combat air patrol position over the carrier. We were there to shoot down bombers or fighters that might come anywhere near us. We also used this time to do some training. When our hour-and-a-half flight was over and it was time to head back, I heard Mooch say, "There's land between us and the ship."

"Land?"

I was pretty sure we hadn't flown over any land. There wasn't any bad weather forecast for that day, but the horizon had completely disappeared. Then I realized that the "land" we were seeing on our radar was sand—a *haboob* in Arabic, a giant sandstorm.

Flying with my fighter squadron, VFA-143, nicknamed the World Famous Pukin' Dogs, circa 1992.

It had completely engulfed the region, and it was likely going to make it a very tough night behind the boat.

As we got closer to the ship, I heard the air traffic controller say, "Salty Dog One Oh Three, three-quarters of a mile, call the ball." He wanted me to confirm I could see the ship's visual landing. I looked outside and saw absolutely nothing. Then I heard the landing signal officer (LSO), who stands on the back of the ship to guide us in, say, "Paddles contact, keep it coming," meaning he could see us even if we couldn't see him. We continued our blind descent toward the ship.

When we were less than a quarter mile away, I could finally see the carrier. At 150 miles per hour, I had about five seconds to line up the airplane to land in the right spot on the flight deck. We touched down. As usual, I went to full power, always necessary in case the landing wasn't successful and I would have to take off again instantly. I expected to feel the comforting pull of the arresting cable bringing us to a stop—but it never came.

"Bolter, bolter, bolter . . . hook skip," called the LSO. To bolter means to fail to catch the arresting cable with the airplane's tailhook. We had to immediately accelerate at full throttle in order to take off again and circle around for another attempt. Off we went back into the sandy darkness of the sky. We came in again, only to experience another bolter. We came around again. Another bolter. We came around again. Now we got a wave-off, meaning our approach was so ugly they wouldn't let me try to land for fear I'd crash. Now I was seriously getting frustrated and nervous.

The visibility was not improving, and we were running out of gas. We went around a number of times more, which only resulted in more wave-offs. Eventually we were "trick or treat," which means we either had to land this time or go get more gas. I boltered again. We were off to the tanker.

The tanker was an A-6 Intruder built with external fuel tanks that circles overhead at three thousand feet, ready to refuel airplanes. Finding the tanker in a sandstorm was a challenge in itself. We were flying by radar only, which was very risky. Once I was within twenty-five feet or so, I was able to see the tanker. I tried not to think about what would happen if I failed. But the bumpiness of the air and my nerves made it take many tries before I finally connected and refueled. Finally, we headed back to the ship to try to land again.

Me and my buddy and squadron mate Jack "Fat Jack" MacDonald, sitting on the inlet of one of our squadron's F-14 Tomcats, circa 1992.

Then I boltered, and boltered again. *I am going to do this for the rest of my life,* I thought. I lost count of how many times I tried to land before I put the airplane down on the deck in the right spot and felt the relief of the arresting cable's tug as we came to an abrupt stop. My right leg was shaking uncontrollably from the adrenaline surging through my system after all those attempts and close calls. Mooch and I made our way off the flight deck and into our brightly lit ready room, the place where the squadron spends time in between flights. The pilots burst into applause when we walked in. They'd been watching our misadventures on a monitor the whole time.

"Welcome back to *Ike*. We never thought we were going to see you fellas again."

I laughed and accepted their congratulations.

A month after returning from the Persian Gulf, on April 25, 1992, Leslie and I got married. And soon after, I applied to U.S. Navy test pilot school in Patuxent River, Maryland. Usually pilots serve in a fleet squadron for four years before applying. I had only been in the Pukin' Dogs for two and a half years, so I didn't think I would be accepted. To my surprise, my brother and I were both selected, so we would be classmates. We started in July 1993.

Leslie and I headed to Patuxent River (everyone calls it Pax River for short), only a few hours from Virginia Beach. This would be the first time in my career that I spent much time with members of the other military services. The school had U.S. Air Force pilots, Marine pilots, Army pilots; there was an Australian F-111 pilot and an Israeli helicopter pilot. Some of the people in my class would later become astronaut colleagues.

Unlike carrier pilots, test pilots fly airplanes before they are certified for use in the regular Navy, to help find and fix any dangerous flaws that could injure or kill the plane's crew. In test pilot school, we learned about aircraft performance, flying qualities, flight control systems, and weapons systems of the aircraft we might be testing. Friday nights we all went out for dinner or gathered at the home of one of my classmates. The weekends we spent studying.

After graduating from test pilot school in July 1994, I moved to the Navy's test squadron for high-performance jet airplanes, located on the same base. My fighter squadron had been a great fraternity, but in some ways the test pilot community was better because of its diversity. There were civilians (a group of people I hadn't previously worked with much in the military), people from different countries, different cultures, ethnicities, sexual orientations, genders, and backgrounds. I was surprised to find that diverse teams were stronger teams, each person bringing their own strengths and perspectives to our shared mission.

My daughter Samantha was born on October 9, 1994, in Pax River. Leslie had a difficult pregnancy, but once Samantha was born, Leslie loved being a mother. She was full of praise and affection, and Samantha was happy, outgoing, and full of fun.

Mark lived near us, and he and his wife came over often, or we would go to their home. I was part of a close-knit group of test pilots and flight test engineers. Leslie and I liked having people around, and my colleagues and friends all liked her. Thanksgivings and Christmases with her family or mine were always great. I was doing the work I wanted to do, and I had a family.

6

ONE AFTERNOON IN early 1995, I was in my cubicle at the test squadron, when I noticed that one of my colleagues had a big stack of papers on his desk. I asked him what he was doing.

"I'm filling out my astronaut application," he said.

I had been planning to fill out an astronaut application someday, but I'd thought I'd need another ten years before I'd be ready. I was only a little more than a year out of test pilot school, and I didn't have a master's degree yet, which I thought was a requirement. But I asked my colleague whether I could take a look at his application. I was curious about what was involved, and I was especially curious about why his stack of papers was so thick. When I paged through it, I saw that NASA was looking for a lot of the kinds of information you would expect: school grades, letters of recommendation, a detailed list of job responsibilities to date. I also noticed that he had included everything he had ever done in his life. This guy was one of the best qualified among us.

Looking over his application, I had an idea: Why not apply and be rejected? It would give me the opportunity to find out what the process was like, and rejection wouldn't harm my chances in the future. I decided to take a different approach from what my colleague had done. I would include only what seemed really important. If my application was short and to the point, maybe the person reading it could take in all the information and be left with a clear sense of who I was. This minimalist approach was also appealing to me because the deadline was fast approaching.

I filled out the application and submitted it on time. Months later, my colleague shared the news that he'd been called for an interview with NASA, in the first week of interviews. It was believed that NASA called their top choices first, and those interviewed in the first round had by far the best chance of being selected. I congratulated him and thought I would never hear anything.

A few weeks later, Mark and his wife were having dinner with Leslie and me at our house. Halfway through the meal, Mark announced that he had also been called for an astronaut interview. I wasn't aware he had even applied.

"That's awesome! Congratulations," I said. And I meant it. I felt he truly deserved it. He was clearly more qualified than I was, with his master's degree in aeronautical engineering. I decided not to mention that I had applied, too, because I figured I wouldn't get an interview anyway, and I didn't want my not getting called to take attention away from his accomplishment.

"I do have a favor to ask you," Mark said. "Do you have a suit I could borrow?"

I did—I had just bought a suit to attend a friend's wedding—so I loaned it to him.

Months later, I came back to the office after flying a test flight and my secretary flagged me down. "Hey, Scott," she said excitedly. "You missed a phone call from Teresa Gomez at NASA." Teresa was the long-serving administrative assistant at the astronaut selection office. Her name was widely known through-out the flight test community; if you got a call from her during the interview process, it was probably good news.

My daughter Samantha and me at the beach at the Naval Air Station Patuxent River in Maryland during my lunch break as a test pilot. She's wearing my navy hat. Circa 1996.

I called back right away, and Teresa asked whether I wanted to come down for an interview. "Yes! Of course," I answered, trying not to shout. "I can come whenever you want."

My interview was scheduled for a couple of weeks later. In the meantime, Mark came back from his own interview feeling that he had done well. He filled me in on exactly what to expect, which was hugely helpful. With Mark's information, I could think about how I would deal with each stage of the daunting process and what answers I might give in the interview. Along with Dave Brown, a fellow Navy pilot who had also interviewed with NASA in the first group, we set up a camera in a conference room at the test pilot school in the evenings to videotape our sessions. Mark and Dave asked me the same questions the committee had asked them. I gave my answers; then they told me what I needed to improve. This was a pretty nice thing for them to do, considering that we were competing against each other.

I reminded Mark that the astronaut selection board had already seen the only suit I owned.

"You have to buy me a new suit," I told him. "It's bad enough that we look exactly the same. We can't wear the exact same thing, too. They won't be able to remember who said what and we'll look stupid."

Mark, being the cheap young Navy lieutenant he was, refused to lay out the money for a new suit. I had to pack the same suit for my interview.

I checked into the hotel near the Johnson Space Center where all the applicants in my group would be staying. The Kings Inn is the same hotel that earlier astronauts stayed in while going through this same process. The interviews and tests would last an entire week, so the interview groups of twenty people got to know one another pretty well. There was definitely a sense of sizing one another up as competition. At the same time, we knew we might also be future colleagues and spaceflight crewmates.

The interview and selection process is incredibly hard. I think they do that on purpose. We were interviewed, we took written tests, and we went through extensive medical testing. We had even more thorough eye exams than in the Navy.

We had all known to expect this. Obviously, astronauts have to be in exceptionally good physical condition and to have as low a risk of developing health problems as possible. Even minor issues could disqualify astronaut hopefuls from flying in space. NASA can't risk an illness in space forcing an early return to Earth or even the death of an astronaut.

The medical tests could cause a lot of anxiety. So many of them were painful, humbling, and embarrassing. We wondered how much we were being tested for toughness as well as for medical issues.

The worst test of all was the one that checked out my lower digestive system. Besides being incredibly painful, what made this procedure more unpleasant was that the doctor needed to pump air into me in order to be able to see my insides. At the end of the test when I was allowed to get up and get dressed, that air remained. I was scheduled for a tour of Space Center Houston right afterward, so I walked over there trying not to expel all that air (and other matter) in an attention-getting way. As with everything else, I wondered whether the challenge not to fart or poop my pants in public was part of the test, to see how we would deal with this kind of discomfort and embarrassment. It's true that life as an astronaut, especially on the space station, has more than its share of physical humiliations.

Finally, I was called in for my interview before an intimidating group of twenty people. John Young, the only astronaut to have commanded four different spacecraft—Gemini, Apollo, the lunar lander from the moon's surface, and the space shuttle—was one of them. He was what you might call an astronaut's astronaut, a living legend. I also recognized Bob Cabana, the chief of the Astronaut Office, and astronauts Jim Wetherbee and Ellen Baker.

John Young was an astronaut's astronaut, flying on the Gemini, Apollo, and space shuttle programs before becoming chief of the Astronaut Office. Here, he drives the Lunar Roving Vehicle (LRV) on the moon during the Apollo 16 mission, April 1972.

I got settled into a chair and tried to sound calm and confident as I greeted them.

"I'm afraid this might all look pretty familiar to you guys," I said, pausing for a laugh. "You've seen this suit before." Then I explained how I had loaned it to my brother, who had been too cheap to buy me a new one. But he did lend me his shoes.

It's risky to try to make a joke in a job interview, but everyone laughed, which made me feel a bit more at ease. They might have been wondering how Mark and I would deal with being twins applying at the same time, and I wanted them to feel they could treat us like any other candidates.

John Young took the lead. He said, simply, "Tell us about your life."

My mind raced. What aspects of my life did he want to hear about? How far back should I go?

"Well, when I graduated from college in 1987—" I began.

"No," Young interrupted. "Go back further. Go back to junior high school."

Later, I would wonder whether they cut off everyone's response and made them start in a different place, to see how they would respond to being interrupted. But at the time, I knew junior high was a bad place to start. I wasn't about to tell them how I used to stare out the window and earn C's. So instead, I told them about fixing up boats with my father, about learning to be an EMT and the experiences I had working on the ambulance. Then I went on to my becoming licensed as a Merchant Marine officer in college, about learning how to work on a ship and how to fly planes and jets, and about the challenges I faced along the way.

As I spoke, I was trying to make my experiences stand out from the other candidates they were seeing. Being a test pilot, as tough as that had been to achieve, wasn't going to set me apart from the other test pilots. But repairing a clunker boat in the open waters of the Atlantic might, or giving a patient CPR on each apartment building landing while I carried her down flights of stairs might.

The official interview lasted around fifty minutes, and I felt that I did well.

Next, we had psychological testing, which I found interesting but stressful, since so much was riding on them. I was tempted to try to figure out what the "right" answer for each question was. The answer to "Do you ever hear voices telling you to do things?" wasn't hard to guess. But "Would you rather steal something from a store or kick a dog?" was trickier. I had to choose one, so I said I would rather steal something. With that type of question, I suspected there was no right or wrong answer.

Then, because an astronaut cannot be claustrophobic, we were each given a heart monitor, zipped into a thick rubber bag not much bigger than a curled-up adult, shut into a closet, and left without any idea of how long we would be in there. For me it was about twenty minutes, and I enjoyed a brief nap.

At the end of the week, we said our good-byes and went home. NASA was to interview six groups in all, and I had been in the third group, so patience would be required.

A few days before Memorial Day weekend, I got a call.

"Scott," the voice said. "This is Dave Leestma." Dave was one of the astronauts I had met in Houston and was the flight crew operations director.

"Yes, sir," I replied.

"Would you like to come fly for us?" he asked. I paused, because I knew that NASA employed a lot of pilots who weren't astronauts. Maybe Dave was asking me to be a pilot, not an astronaut.

"Uh, maybe," I said. "Fly what?"

He answered with a laugh. "The space shuttle, of course."

I felt humbled by the role I was being asked to step into.

"I'd love to," I said. "Have you called my brother yet?"

Waiting to find out whether Mark was selected was almost as suspenseful as waiting to hear about my own fate.

"I just got off the phone with him," Dave answered. "Yeah, he got selected, too."

This was the first time NASA had selected relatives. We'd been concerned they might not want to select brothers, especially twins, and in the back of my mind, I had been thinking that they might choose one of us and not the other.

"Mark actually asked me about you, too, and I told him I was about to call you," Dave said. So my brother knew that I was to become an astronaut before I did. That was fine with me.

I hung up the phone after talking to Dave, and I told Leslie: "I'm going to be an astronaut." She was thrilled for me. Next I called my brother, and we spent a few minutes on the phone congratulating each other and talking about our moving plans. I got on the phone with my parents and they were overwhelmed by the news. Word spread quickly within our small family—the next time we saw our maternal grandmother, she had had a custom bumper sticker made for her car that read, MY TWIN GRANDSONS ARE ASTRONAUTS. I would imagine people thought she was crazy.

The next day, I told my colleagues that I had been chosen to be an astronaut. They were all so thrilled, their excitement actually helped it to sink in for me what I had achieved. My life had just changed. I was going to have the chance to fly in space.

When the press found out that NASA had selected Mark and me, they called the astronaut selection office to ask about it. A reporter asked Duane Ross, who ran the astronaut selection office, "Did you know you picked two brothers?"

His answer: "No, we picked two very accomplished test pilots who happen to be twins."

Me ready to transition from test pilot to astronaut. Circa 1996.

PART 2

SPACE

My astronaut class photo, 1996. We were known as the Sardines because there were so many of us—the largest class in NASA history. We were all Americans, except as labeled below. From left to right and back row to front: Christer Fuglesang (Sweden), John Herrington, Steve MacLean (Canada), Peggy Whitson, Steve Frick, Duane Carey, Dan Tani, Heidemarie Stefanyshyn-Piper, Jeff Williams, Don Pettit, Philippe Perrin (France), Dan Burbank, Mike Massimino, Lee Morin, Piers Sellers, John Phillips, Rick Mastracchio, Christopher Loria, Paul Lockhart, Charlie Hobaugh, Willie McCool, Pedro Duque (Spain), Soichi Noguchi (Japan), Mamoru Mohri (Japan), Gerhard Thiele (Germany), Mark Polansky, Sandy Magnus, Paul Richards, Yvonne Cagle, Jim Kelly, Pat Forrester, Dave Brown, Umberto Guidoni (Italy), Mike Fincke, Stephanie Wilson, Julie Payette (Canada), Lisa Nowak, Frank Caldeiro, Mark, Laurel Clark, Rex Walheim, me, Joan Higginbotham, and Charlie Camarda.

7

ONE HOT DAY in early July 1996, Leslie and I packed up our two cars and left Pax River for Houston. Samantha, almost two now, was an adorable toddler. We found a house we liked quickly and moved in on August 1. Mark and his family moved to town a little after we did.

On the Friday night before our official Monday start date, we went to a party where we met all of our new classmates. We were ASCANs, short for "astronaut candidates." (We would become full-fledged astronauts the first time we left the Earth's atmosphere.) It wasn't until that party that I learned our class would include international astronauts. There were thirty-five Americans and nine astronauts from other countries, which made us the largest astronaut class in NASA history. I met so many people that night—not only my classmates, but their spouses and significant others, astronauts from previous classes, *their* partners, and other NASA people. It was exciting to know that we were going to be such a big part of one another's lives, and maybe spend time in space together.

Our training started out in classrooms, where all forty-four of us began to realize how much we needed to learn. We heard lectures on geology, meteorology, physics, oceanography, and aerodynamics. We learned about the history of NASA. We learned about the T-38, the jet aircraft astronauts fly to train for spaceflight.

Most of all, we learned all about the space shuttle—how each system worked, what could go wrong with them, and how we could fix those problems. Then we moved on to the shuttle mission simulator. This was designed to give us the experience of flying the shuttle from the safety of the ground. Our trainers tested us with malfunctions and disasters we could face during a real flight.

By far the hardest part of shuttle training was liftoff and the climb into space, called ascent. We had to train for every possible problem that may happen during this stage and know how to fix them. This phase of flight training revealed those who had learned their stuff and those who hadn't. We also trained hard for the orbit phase, since that was where we would spend the most time on a real mission, and for deorbit prep—taking an orbiting spaceship and turning it into a space plane we could land. As a pilot, I practiced reentry and landing thousands of times. We never stopped practicing. This is the moment in the mission when having something go wrong can be the most serious, so I had to be prepared to deal with anything.

The very complexity of the space shuttle was why I wanted to fly it. But learning these systems and practicing in the simulators showed me how much more complicated this spacecraft was than anything I could have imagined. There were more than two thousand switches and circuit breakers in the cockpit, more than a million parts, and almost as many ways for me to mess up.

The Astronaut Office was a busy place in those days. Some

very experienced astronauts were still around, and it was an honor to serve along with them. John Glenn was assigned to a space shuttle flight not long after I became an astronaut. Glenn, who had been the first American to orbit the Earth, was returning to space in his late seventies to study how spaceflight impacts aging bodies.

John Glenn Jr., the first American astronaut to orbit the Earth, returned to space for shuttle mission STS-95 at age seventy-seven, becoming the oldest astronaut to fly in space. October 1998.

One day I had four-year-old Samantha with me, and as I was walking her around, I saw Glenn hard at work in his office. I introduced myself and Samantha.

He looked up and said, "Hi, young lady. What are you doing today?"

"I'm going to lunch with my dad," Samantha answered.

"What's your favorite food?" he asked her.

"Macaroni and cheese," she said.

Glenn gave her a look of pleased surprise. He held up the papers he had been working on.

"Look right here," he said. "I was just selecting my space food for my mission and I just wrote, 'Macaroni and cheese.' That's my favorite, too!"

Another time, I had Samantha with me at a party, and I encouraged her to talk to John Young about his experience walking on the moon. Samantha approached him and said, "My dad says you walked on the moon."

John responded, "I didn't *walk* on the moon. I *worked* on the moon!"

More than a year later, we were watching a documentary about Apollo, and I pointed out John Young to Samantha. "You met him, remember? He walked on the moon."

Samantha didn't miss a beat: "Daddy, he didn't walk on the moon—he *worked* on the moon."

After John Glenn completed his mission, in October 1998, I inherited his parking space and used it for the next eighteen years.

As part of my ASCAN training, I learned to fly the Shuttle Training Aircraft (STA), a Gulfstream business jet that had been changed to come as close to the reality of landing the space shuttle as possible. The STA flew out of El Paso, Texas, so we would fly over there in a T-38, which took a little over an hour.

In El Paso one day in March 1999, I had just finished my ten practice landings in the STA and was getting ready to fly back to Houston when one of the senior shuttle commanders, Curt Brown, came up to me. His experience—five shuttle missions in six years—was nearly unequaled. But he also had the reputation of being unfriendly to those he considered not worthy of his attention.

"Hey, come over here," he said sternly. "I need to talk to you."

I followed him into a private office, wondering what I had done to annoy him. He shut the door behind us, then turned and poked me in the chest three times while staring straight into my eyes.

"You better have your act together," he said to me, "because we're flying in space in six months."

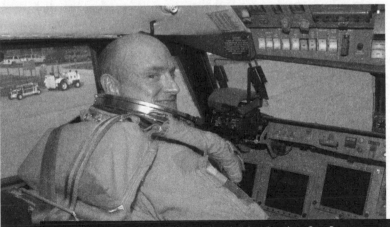

I was flying in the STA, training to pilot the shuttle, when Curt Brown surprised me with the news that I'd be on his shuttle mission—my first time going to space. March 1999.

I felt a couple of different things at once. One was: *I'm going to space in six months!*

Another was: *Wow, what a terrible way to let someone know he's got his first flight assignment.*

"Yes, sir," I said. "I'll have my act together."

Curt told me to keep this news a secret. I told my brother, of course.

Curt would command mission STS-103 on space shuttle *Discovery*. It was an emergency repair mission to the Hubble Space Telescope, and we would be joined by French astronaut Jean-François Clervoy (we called him "Billy Bob," since "Jean-François" didn't sound very Texan), John Grunsfeld, Mike Foale, Steve Smith, and Claude Nicollier. I was to be the only rookie on the crew and the first American in my class to fly. The mission would include four spacewalks, each more than eight hours long.

The Hubble Space Telescope has been making observations of the universe since 1990. Until then, astronomers could never get a truly clear view of the night sky because of the distorting effect of the atmosphere. Observing stars and galaxies through that filter was like trying to read a book underwater. Putting a telescope in orbit outside the atmosphere and past the reach of light pollution has enabled scientists to make discoveries about how fast the universe is expanding, how old it is, and what it is made of.

Hubble has helped us to discover new planets in new solar systems and confirmed the existence of dark energy and dark matter. This one scientific instrument has revolutionized what we know about our universe. So the task of repairing it—which always brings the risk of damaging or even destroying its sensitive components—is an enormous responsibility.

Eileen Collins became the first woman to command a space shuttle mission, on *Columbia*, in July 1999. Once that flight got off the ground, our *Discovery* mission crew would become the prime crew, our launch date set for October 14, 1999. But there was a problem on *Columbia* during ascent. An electrical short disabled the center engine's digital control unit. The engine continued to operate on its backup—but something had gone seriously wrong, and NASA needed to find out what. The *Columbia* mission was cut short. When the shuttle was safely back on the ground, an investigation was begun.

It was revealed that wiring in the payload bay had been rubbing against an exposed screw. It was a good reminder to everyone of how little it can take to cause a disaster. Further inspections revealed deteriorating wiring throughout the space shuttle fleet that would need to be fixed before any of the shuttles could fly again. That caused a delay in our launch date to November 19. As inspections and repairs to the wiring dragged on, we were delayed further, to December 2, then to December 6.

These delays were frustrating for everyone. But finally, the day after Thanksgiving, we said our good-byes and went into quarantine. NASA's quarantines isolated space travelers from germs before a launch in order to decrease the chances of us getting sick in space.

We didn't have a lot to do once we were in quarantine. We had our checklists to review. We had some equipment to learn. We had to sign crew photos to hand out to people who worked on the mission, at least a thousand of them. At the end of our workday, which was actually in the morning, we watched movies together.

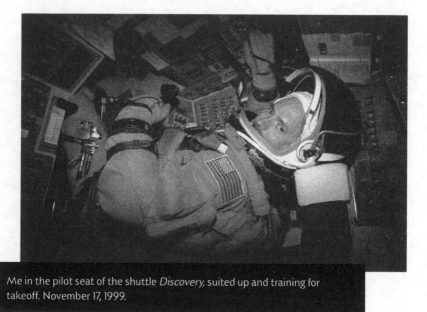

Me in the pilot seat of the shuttle *Discovery*, suited up and training for takeoff. November 17, 1999.

While we were in quarantine, our launch date changed again, from December 6 to December 11. It was mildly annoying, but we all understood that delays were part of spaceflight. Then we were delayed again, to December 16. By the morning of the six-teenth, we had been in quarantine for twenty days and were get-ting tired of it. We were ready to go to space or go home. Then the launch was delayed until December 17, when inspectors had found a possible problem with a weld in the external tank.

The morning of the seventeenth, I woke up and looked at the weather forecast—cloudy, raining, and possibly even lightning.

But the weather at Cape Canaveral could change quickly, so the countdown continued. Workers began filling the external tank, a process that takes hours. We got suited up and headed out to the launchpad. It seemed we might finally be going to space. We got strapped into our seats and started preparing the space shuttle to launch as we got closer to our planned liftoff time of 8:47 p.m.

There are a few "holds" built into the countdown—points where extra time has been allowed so we can stop the clock and make sure everything is being done right without being rushed. One of these holds is at T-minus nine minutes, and it's the last chance to decide whether we are "go" or not. We kept at the T-minus nine hold for a long time, up to our planned launch time and past it. At 8:52 p.m., the launch director made the decision to scrub, or cancel, due to weather. We would try again the next day.

On December 18, we scrubbed again, this time before we suited up. At this point, we had been in quarantine twenty-two days. Because I was launching for the first time, I had invited practically everyone I knew to come to Florida, along with their friends, about eight hundred people in all, and with every delay the group got smaller as people changed their travel plans.

Jim Wetherbee, an astronaut who was serving as the director of flight crew operations, came by to talk to us. We all sat around a conference table together, and Jim said, "We're going to knock this thing off and try again in the new year." It was now a week before Christmas, and NASA had decided to give the ground crew a chance to go home to their families for the holidays. We were also coming up against another type of conflict: NASA wanted us safely back on Earth before January 1, 2000, because there was so much anxiety about the Y2K computer glitch, and not every NASA facility was Y2K compliant yet.

All of my crewmates seemed pleased—they wanted to go home. I was the only one who didn't want to see the launch postponed. I had come here with the expectation of going to space, and I didn't want to give that up and wait weeks before we actually launched. We packed up our things, prepared to head back to Houston, until an hour later NASA changed their minds again. The launch was back on for tomorrow.

I was the only one who was happy, because I was the only one who had never been to space before.

8

THE NEXT DAY, December 19, as promised, we got suited up for launch. The weather was only 60 percent go, but the countdown continued throughout the day. Several hours before the scheduled launch time of 7:50 p.m., we left the Operations and Checkout Building and waved to the media as we walked to the Astrovan, an Airstream motor home that is used just for carrying astronauts the nine miles to the launch site. The space shuttle, fully loaded with liquid oxygen and hydrogen, was essentially a giant bomb, so when it was fueled, the area was cleared of people. As we approached the launchpad, which usually bustled with hundreds of workers, we saw that it was eerily abandoned.

We rode the elevator in the launch tower up to the 195-foot level, and Curt entered the orbiter first. The cryogenic fuel created condensation that froze into snow, so even though the weather was warm, some of us had a brief snowball fight. Others used the bathroom known affectionately as the Last Toilet on Earth.

Next we entered the White Room one by one, a sterile space around the hatch. When it was my turn, I got into the harnesses for my parachute and fitted the comm cap on my head, a small leather cap that contains the speakers and mic for the spacesuit's communication system. Then I kneeled just inside the hatchway while the closeout crew removed the galoshes that kept us from tracking dirt into the spacecraft. Inside the cockpit, everything was pointing up at the sky, so I had to crawl across the ladder, rather than up, in order to get to my seat, which felt like it was hanging off the ceiling. I managed to pull myself up and shimmy into position on my parachute, an uncomfortable bulk under my back. The closeout crew guys, including my friend and astronaut classmate Dave Brown, strapped us into our seats as tightly as they could and helped us get all our connections hooked up— comm, cooling, and oxygen.

We were positioned on our backs for launch, with our knees above our heads, looking straight up at the sky. The position was uncomfortable, especially once we were tightly strapped in.

The preparation for launch was one of the busiest times for the pilot. I was responsible for getting many of the systems ready prior to flight, which meant flipping the right switches and circuit breakers, starting motors and pumps, and connecting electrical circuits. There were many ways I could mess things up so we wouldn't be able to go to space today. And there were many ways I could mess things up so we'd never go anywhere ever again. I needed to be *so* careful—but not so careful that I got behind the timeline. If certain things weren't done correctly by the right point in the countdown, the launch couldn't proceed.

The countdown clock stopped for the T-minus nine hold. Soon this sixteen-story structure was going to lift off the Earth in a controlled explosion. For a moment I thought, *Boy, this is a really dumb thing to be doing.*

I had been told that astronauts flying in the space shuttle had

The shuttle *Discovery* waits on the launchpad for takeoff. November 13, 1999.

a risk of death similar to that of Allied infantrymen on D-day. I knew how the crew of *Challenger* had died, and I understood that I was now taking the same risks. I wasn't scared, but I felt aware of those risks, all at once.

We had been waiting several hours by this point, long enough for some of us to have to use the diaper we wore under our pressure suits. When the first American to go to space, Alan Shepard, was waiting to launch, a number of technical delays forced him to wait so long that he needed to use the bathroom. He was told to simply go inside his pressure suit, so the first American to leave the Earth did so with wet pants. Ever since, most astronauts have worn diapers or a urine collection device. I can't believe I'm back in diapers again for the most daring and exciting moment in my life so far—but it's better than having to pee my pants!

Eventually the countdown clock reached the last minute. At thirty seconds, the space shuttle computers took over the launch count. At six seconds, the three main engines roared to life with a million pounds of thrust, but we didn't go anywhere because the shuttle was bolted to the launchpad by eight giant bolts. At zero, the solid rocket boosters ignited and the bolts were exploded in half, setting the shuttle free. We leaped off the launchpad with 7 million pounds of thrust.

I knew from watching videos and from seeing launches in person that the shuttle appeared to rise very slowly at first. Inside, though, there wasn't a thing about it that felt slow. One second we were sitting on the launchpad, completely still, and the next we were being hurtled straight up faster than would have seemed possible, being shaken violently in every direction. We went from a standstill to faster than the speed of sound in less than a minute.

There wasn't much for the commander and pilot to do at this stage other than monitor the systems to make sure everything was going as it should, and to be prepared to respond if it didn't. People sometimes mistakenly imagined that we were "flying" the shuttle, that our hands were on the controls and that we could move *Discovery* around in the sky if we wanted to, like an airplane. In fact, as long as those solid rocket boosters were burning, we were all essentially just along for the ride. The boosters can't be throttled or shut down.

Once the solid rockets dropped off, two minutes after we left the launchpad, we were flying on the power of the three main engines, so now there was more we could do to control our fates. We continued to monitor all the systems closely as we traveled higher and faster. For the first two minutes, we were prepared for the possibility that if something went seriously wrong—most likely a main engine failure—we could turn around and land on the runway at the Kennedy Space Center. We called this abort mode "return to launch site" (RTLS), and it required the shuttle to fly Mach seven backward. No one had ever tried this and no one wanted to. So we were all happy when we got to the point known as "negative return," when RTLS was no longer a possibility and we had other, less risky abort options.

As the shuttle burned through its propellants, it got lighter, increasing its acceleration. When the acceleration got to 3 g's (at 3 g's a 200-pound person feels like they weigh 600 pounds), it became difficult to breathe; the parachute and oxygen bottles I wore on my back in case of emergency pulled on the straps on my chest.

As we accelerated, Curt and I, with Billy Bob's assistance,

monitored the performance of all the systems so we could be ready at a split second's notice if we needed to take corrective actions.

When the shuttle gets to its planned orbit, we reach the moment called MECO—pronounced "mee-ko," which stands for "main engine cut off"—when the now-nearly-empty external tank separated to burn up in the atmosphere. MECO was a great moment because it meant we'd survived the launch phase, one of the riskiest of our entire mission. We had accelerated from zero to 17,500 miles per hour in just eight and a half minutes. Now we were floating in space. I looked out the window and saw something so incredible it was difficult to comprehend. I tapped Curt on the shoulder and pointed outside. "Hey, what's that?" I asked him.

"That's the sunrise," said Curt.

An orbital sunrise, my first. I had no idea how many more of these I was going to see. I've now seen thousands, and their beauty has never waned.

I unstrapped myself from my seat and floated headfirst through the passageway to the mid-deck, enjoying the strange sensation of weightlessness. When I got there, I found two guys with their heads in puke bags. They were experienced astronauts, but some people have to get used to space every time they go. I'm very lucky that I don't suffer from the nausea and dizziness that some people do.

Once we got to orbit, I had to adjust to living in such small quarters with six other people. There were two "floors" in the shuttle, the flight deck and the mid-deck, and each of them was smaller than the inside of a minivan. We worked, ate, went to the bathroom, and slept on top of one another. At least our eight-day mission would be one of the shorter ones; the longest space shuttle mission was seventeen days.

On our second full day in space, we reached the Hubble Space Telescope. It's in a much higher orbit than most satellites—150 miles higher than the space station—making missions to it riskier than flights to a lower orbit.

Billy Bob moved into high gear once we were safely in orbit. He was always excited about what we were doing, always enthusiastic, and always had time to help me out. He taught me all the little details about how to live and work in space that they can't really teach you on the ground, like moving around in zero g, organizing your workspace when everything floats, and of course fun things like peeing while upside down—lessons I would later pass on to others when I became more experienced.

Billy Bob was also not above pranking me. I was still the rookie, after all. When I went into my clothing locker to get changed, I discovered that I had only one pair of underwear for the entire mission. Billy Bob had hidden the rest. I think he expected me to panic, but the joke was on him; I didn't really care. Wearing the same underwear for days was actually good training for my year in space.

One thing that surprised me about living in space was that it was hard to focus. Part of it was being in space for the first time—who could concentrate on a checklist while floating with the beautiful Earth turning just outside the window? But beyond that, basic tasks were much harder in zero g. I learned that everything was just going to take a bit more time.

There were physical effects, too. Feeling the fluid in my

body move to my head for the first time was odd and at times uncomfortable. All astronauts experience some level of difficulty concentrating on a short mission—what we call "space brain"— and I was no exception. After you've been in space for weeks or months, you adjust. I couldn't afford to let my work suffer, though, because there would be serious consequences if I messed something up.

On day three, Steve Smith and John Grunsfeld took their first spacewalk, successfully replacing the gyroscopes in the Hubble Space Telescope. The following day, Mike Foale and Claude Nicollier performed their spacewalk, replacing Hubble's central computer and a fine-guidance sensor. On day six, Steve and John went outside again, this time to install a transmitter and a solid-state recorder. There had been a fourth planned spacewalk, but it was canceled in order to get us back on Earth before Y2K.

Me in the pilot seat during my first spaceflight. December 1999.

Day seven of the mission, the next-to-last day, marked the first time a space shuttle would be spending Christmas in orbit (and, it turns out, the last).

That night, everyone gathered for dinner on the mid-deck. Billy Bob showed me some special French gourmet food he had brought up with him. We heated it up and took it up to the flight deck. We turned the lights off and played some Mozart, watching the beautiful Earth turning below us while we ate this fantastic food and reflected on how lucky we were to be celebrating Christmas as no one on the space shuttle had done before.

When it was time to go home, I decided to get Billy Bob back for pranking me by hiding the long underwear we layer under the pressure suits for reentry. He didn't suspect anything when he started getting dressed. Then he began tossing through his bag of gear again and again, a look of alarm on his face. Once he was thoroughly distressed, thinking he wouldn't be able to get dressed in time for landing, I finally took pity on him and gave it back.

The landing phase was the most challenging for the commander and pilot. When the space shuttle hit the outer atmosphere at 17,500 miles per hour, the resulting friction created heat of more than 3,000 degrees Fahrenheit. We had to do everything right and trust that the insulating tiles on the space shuttle would protect us.

For about twelve minutes, hot ionized gases built up around the spacecraft. Once we got farther down into the atmosphere and the air became thicker, the space shuttle's airplane design became crucial. Up to that point, it could have been shaped like a capsule, but now Curt was going to land this spaceship in the dark on a runway at the Kennedy Space Center. The space shuttle was hard to land because it had no engines that would allow us to pull up and try a second landing if need be. While Curt had the controls, I also had a lot of responsibilities as pilot, a role similar to the copilot of an airplane—monitoring the shuttle's systems, giving information to Curt, lowering the landing gear, and opening the drag chute, the parachute that slows us down once we are on the runway.

I lowered the landing gear at the right moment, and soon after, we heard an alarm: a tire pressure sensor was warning us that we might have a blown tire. The space shuttle's tires were specially designed to survive launch, a week or two orbiting in a vacuum, and landing at incredibly high speed. If one of them had blown out, our landing could be a disaster. As the alarm kept sounding, I encouraged Curt to ignore the tire pressure—there was nothing we could do about it, and he needed to focus on the landing.

He nailed the landing, the tires held under us, and we rolled to a stop. "Nice landing!" I told him, completing one of my most important responsibilities of the whole mission.

I was surprised by how dizzy I felt being back in Earth's gravity. When I tried to unstrap myself from my seat and get up, I found I nearly couldn't move. I felt like I weighed a thousand pounds. We climbed from the space shuttle to a converted motor home where we could change out of our launch-and-entry suits and get a brief medical examination. Trying to get out of the suit worsened my dizziness, and the world spun like a carnival ride.

We were taken back to the crew quarters at Kennedy, where we were able to shower before meeting with our families and friends. I went out that night to Fishlips, a seafood restaurant in Cape Canaveral, with everyone who had come for my landing. It was a bit unreal, sitting at a long table enjoying fish tacos, when just a few hours earlier I had been hurtling toward the Earth at a blistering speed in a 3,000-degree fireball. A couple of days later, I was back in the office, a real astronaut.

Jean-Francois Clervoy, also known as Billy Bob, sports a New Year's Eve party hat after *Discovery* lands back on Earth. December 28, 1999.

9

AS MY LIFE was returning to normal following my first space-flight, I wondered what would come next. Soon after we came back from our mission, NASA was looking for a new director of operations (DOR)—an astronaut who lived in Star City, just out-side Moscow, and connected the U.S. and Russian space agencies. The DOR dealt with the details of training American astronauts to fly on Russian spacecraft and served as the on-site leader for the U.S. astronauts training there. The International Space Station was still in the early stages of construction, and we were ramping up to train international crews in Houston and Star City, as well as in Europe and Japan. I was asked to serve as DOR. I was flattered, but I was reluctant to take the job. I thought of myself as a shuttle astronaut, a pilot, not a space station guy. I told my brother in private that I didn't want to get that space station stink on me, think-ing it would be hard to get off, resulting in fewer shuttle flights.

Still, when I was offered the job, I accepted it. My approach to any unwanted assignment had always been to express my misgiv-ings and my preferences. But then if I was still asked to take the hard job, I did my best to make it a success.

A few months later, my crewmate Mike Foale flew with me to Russia to help because he spoke fluent Russian and had experience working there. We were met at the airport by a Russian driver named Ephim, a squat, gruff bull of a man. Ephim loaded us into a Chevy Astro van, one of the few Western vehicles in Russia at the time, and I watched Moscow go by as we passed through the city. Soon we were passing through the gates of Star City.

Star City is the Russian equivalent of the Johnson Space Center; it's the place where the Russian cosmonauts have been trained for the last fifty years. There is a giant statue of Yuri Gagarin, who became the first human in space in 1961, taking a simple, humble step forward while holding a bouquet of flowers behind his back. Years ago, the Russian space agency built NASA an awkward row of Western-style town houses especially for us Americans called "the cottages." Staying in them is sort of like staying on a movie set based on a Russian idea of how Americans live. There are huge fridges and huge TVs, but somehow everything is slightly off.

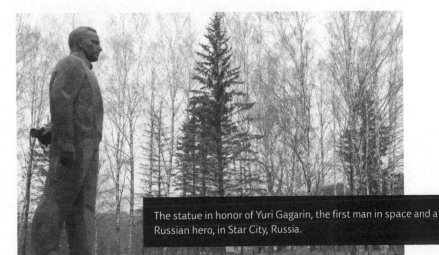

The statue in honor of Yuri Gagarin, the first man in space and a Russian hero, in Star City, Russia.

The next morning, I had to get up very early for a four-hour ride on a bumpy road in a bus that smelled of burning engine oil. We headed to Russa, the remote village where space flyers trained in case the Soyuz—the Russian space capsule that brings astronauts and cosmonauts to the ISS and back—lands in cold weather. The plan was for me to participate in the Russian winter survival training.

During the reign of Ivan the Terrible, Russa had been a thriving city, but now, having been largely destroyed in World War II, there wasn't much there. I joined American astronaut Doug Wheelock and cosmonaut Dmitri (Dima) Kondratyev as a three-man crew. I didn't know yet that I would wind up flying in space with both of them much later in my career. Doug was an Army officer and helicopter pilot, even-tempered and easy to get along with. Dima was a fighter pilot who had flown the MiG-29. Before the end of the Cold War, Dima and I might have faced each other in air-to-air combat. In fact, years later we figured out that we were once stationed on opposite lines of the Soviet border in Scandinavia, him protecting the Russian Bear bombers and me in the F-14 Tomcat protecting the aircraft carrier battle group.

The survival training was grueling. We were sent out to a field with a used Soyuz capsule to practice what we would do after a remote landing, equipped with nothing but the emergency supplies carried in the spacecraft. Dima didn't speak much English, and neither Doug nor I spoke great Russian, but the three of us communicated well enough to get through the training. On the last day, we hiked through the woods, a navigation exercise to simulate meeting up with rescue forces. The landscape was stunning, with birch trees stark against the sky and everything covered with fresh sparkling snow. We emerged from the forest onto a large frozen lake that was steaming in the subzero temperatures, dotted with old Russian men sitting on their pails, ice fishing. This image struck me as serene and quintessentially Russian, like an epic scene from the film *Doctor Zhivago*. It was a moving sight that will be etched in my memory forever.

Working in Russia as DOR was a big transition. NASA and Roscosmos, the Russian space agency, were still figuring out how to train international crews together to work on an international space station. Building a space station was a huge undertaking with a lot of potential for power struggles, cultural conflicts, and temper tantrums from big egos on both sides.

It was hard to develop a smooth relationship between the Russians and Americans. We had different languages, different technology, and different ideas about the best way to fly in space. But I liked the Russians I met and took a real interest in their culture and history. This built the foundation for our future collaboration on the International Space Station.

The first module, or section, of the ISS was a Russian module called the FGB (*funktsionalno-gruzovoy blok*, functional cargo block). It was launched in November 1998, followed two weeks later by Node 1, the first U.S. module, which was taken into space on space shuttle *Endeavour*. When the two modules were joined together, it was a major international accomplishment. The infant space station wasn't ready to be permanently occupied, though, because it lacked necessary features like a life support system, a kitchen, and a toilet. It orbited empty for the next year and a half until the addition of the Russian service module, which added those essential systems that made it habitable.

In late October 2000, I traveled to Baikonur for the launch of Expedition 1, the first long-duration mission to the ISS. Bill Shepherd would be launching on a Soyuz with two Russian cosmonauts, Yuri Gidzenko and Sergei Krikalev. This would be only the second time an American was traveling on a Soyuz. Another three-person crew would be replacing them in March. It was hard to believe that the station would be occupied nonstop from then on. Since I still thought of myself as a space shuttle guy, I didn't think I would fly a long-duration flight on station myself. I hoped to be assigned to another shuttle mission soon, as pilot again. Then, if I was lucky, I might fly two more space shuttle missions as commander, and that would probably be the end of my spaceflight career. I found it impossible to imagine that I would live on the space station one day, let alone for nearly a year.

The following year, I came back from Russia, and soon after, Charlie Precourt, the head of the Astronaut Office, asked me to serve as backup to Peggy Whitson for Expedition 5 to ISS, to launch in June 2002. My first reaction was to hesitate. A mission to the International Space Station was very different from being a shuttle pilot. And piloting a rocket ship was what made me want to be an astronaut in the first place.

"If I'm being honest, I'm not sure whether I ever want to spend six months on the space station. I'm a pilot," I told Charlie. "I'm not a mission specialist. Science really isn't my thing."

Charlie understood; he was a pilot, too. He offered me a deal.

If I would serve as Peggy's backup, which would mean returning to Russia for a long period of time to train on the Russian ISS systems and on the Soyuz, he would assign me as commander of the space shuttle on my next flight, and as the commander of the International Space Station after that.

"Okay," I said somewhat grudgingly.

I had been given this assignment later than normal, so I had to play catch-up. I trained a great deal in Russia, learning their Soyuz and the Russian part of the ISS. I also worked on my Russian language skills, which I had always found painfully hard. I had to learn the U.S. part of the space station, too, which is incredibly complex; how to fly the space station's robotic arm; and how to do spacewalks.

I went through Russian water survival training with Dima Kondratyev, whom I had already gone through winter survival training with, and cosmonaut Sasha Kaleri, my two new backup crewmates. We left early in the morning on September 11, 2001, on an old Russian Navy vessel from Sochi, a coastal town that would later host the Olympics in 2014. As we slowly motored out to sea, we were given a tour of the ship and shown how to use some of the equipment. Toilet paper was forbidden, as it clogged up the sanitation system. We were told instead to use a brush soaking in antiseptic next to the toilet. *Great,* I thought.

The water survival training wasn't much more pleasant than winter survival training. An old Soyuz was lowered into the water, and we had to climb into it wearing our launch-and-entry suits, called Sokol suits. The hatch was closed behind us, and we sat there in the stifling heat until we were told to remove our Sokol suits and put on our winter survival gear, followed by a rubber anti-exposure suit. It was so tight inside the Soyuz that Dima, Sasha, and I had to take turns lying spread out across one another's laps to struggle out of one suit and into the other. The capsule heaved up and down with the rolling swells of the Black Sea, and I thought about how impossible this would be if we were returning from space and already weakened from living in zero gravity. Once in my winter clothing—even though the Soyuz was as hot as a sauna—I then had to put on the full rubber anti-exposure suit, including layers of hats and hoods. We were drenched in our own sweat and exhausted even before climbing out of the Soyuz and jumping into the sea. Like winter survival training, this was mostly a team-building exercise in dealing with shared hardship.

Me being helped out of the Soyuz training capsule after water survival training. September 2001.

Once we finished up our training, we headed back to the bridge of the ship, where the captain toasted our success. I thought about how strange this scene would have been even just a few years before—me, an officer in the United States Navy, on the bridge of a Russian Navy ship with its captain and Dima, a Russian Air Force pilot.

As we got back on shore, we got a call from Star City telling us that two planes had just crashed into the twin towers of the World Trade Center in New York City. We were as shocked as the rest of the world, and for me it was a horrible feeling to be so far from my country when it was under attack. We found the nearest television, and like most people at home, I spent hours watching the news. The Russians did everything they could to help us. They brought food, translated the Russian news so we could understand what was going on, and even canceled the remaining training to get us back home as soon as possible. We flew out of Sochi the next day, and I was startled by how much the security had increased at the airport, despite the fact that the terrorist attack had been in another country on the other side of the world. As we waited in Moscow for flights to the United States to resume, we saw flowers piled high outside the gate of the U.S. embassy in a show of solidarity that I will never forget.

10

PEGGY WHITSON'S LAUNCH went off without a hitch in June 2002, and soon after I was assigned to be the commander of my second space shuttle mission, STS-118, tasked with delivering new hardware to the International Space Station. The mission would be twelve days long, and we were scheduled to fly on space shuttle *Columbia* in October 2003. Charlie Precourt had been true to his word.

Since this was only my second shuttle flight, and I hadn't yet been to the ISS, the new chief astronaut wanted my pilot to be someone who had spaceflight experience. The only available pilots were Charlie Hobaugh, Mark Polansky, and my brother. Of these, I thought my brother was the best fit: we got along and we understood each other. But if Mark and I were to fly in space together, we would have to accept the possibility that our children could lose both their dad and their uncle all at once. The more I thought about it, the less I thought it was a good idea.

I was down to two candidates. Mark Polansky didn't want to fly as my pilot, since he technically had more experience than I did. That left "Scorch"—Charlie Hobaugh. Scorch told me he didn't mind flying with a classmate as his commander because he appreciated any opportunity to fly in space. Because he had a reputation for speaking his mind, I knew he meant it.

So my crew was set: Scorch would be my pilot, and the rest of the crew would be rounded out by five mission specialists: Tracy Caldwell, Barbara Morgan, Lisa Nowak, Scott Parazynski, and Dave Williams.

On the morning of February 1, 2003, I was standing on my front lawn looking north. It was a Saturday, just before nine a.m., and shuttle mission *Columbia* with seven of my colleagues, including three of my classmates, was returning to Earth. I thought I might be able to see the streak of fire as *Columbia* entered the atmosphere north of Houston on its way to land at the Kennedy Space Center. It was foggy, but as I watched the sky, I saw a bright flash in a break in the fog. *Columbia!* I went back inside, and as it got closer to the planned landing time, I started paying more attention to NASA TV. I noticed Charlie Hobaugh in the control center—and I saw he was slouching low in his chair. That was a strange sight for a squared-away Marine like him. Then I heard Charlie say, "*Columbia*, Houston, comm check." A long pause went by. There wasn't an answer. This wasn't normal.

Charlie spoke again. "*Columbia*, Houston. Comm check. *Columbia*, Houston. UHF comm check." He had switched to the backup comm system. Still no response from *Columbia*. My heart started beating faster. The countdown clock got down to zero and started to count up. *Columbia* was supposed to be on the ground by now. Charlie kept making the same call over and over again. I jumped in my car and headed to the space center, dialing my brother on my cell phone. My call woke him up. By then reports were coming in that pieces of the orbiter were falling about a hundred miles north of Houston.

It soon became clear what had gone wrong. The space shuttle's external tank, which was sort of like an enormous orange thermos, was covered with foam to help insulate the cryogenic propellant inside and keep ice from forming on the surface. Almost from the start of the shuttle program, the vibration of launch caused pieces of foam to fall off the tank. Engineers had been unable to completely solve the issue. Usually the foam fell in small enough bits that there was little damage. But the day *Columbia* launched, a large piece of foam had fallen, struck the left wing, and damaged the heat shield. There had been a discussion on the ground, and the team had quickly concluded there was no problem. The crew of *Columbia* was told about the foam strike, and that there was "absolutely no concern for entry."

Apollo veteran John Young, commander of the first space shuttle mission and conscience of the Astronaut Office, was always standing up in our Monday-morning meetings, trying to convince people of the danger posed by the foam. I remember him saying distinctly, "We have to do something about this or a crew is going to die."

I thought about the people I knew who had been on *Columbia*. I had known Dave Brown since he'd been at Pax River with me. He had helped Mark prepare for his NASA interview and then helped me when I was called. That was the type of guy he was.

Laurel Clark was a Navy doctor before she became an astronaut, and our families had become close soon after we moved to

The *Columbia* disaster was both a professional and personal loss for me, having friends and colleagues among the crew members killed. The crew, from left to right: Michael Anderson, Rick Husband, Laurel Clark, Willie McCool, Ilan Ramon, Kalpana Chawla, and David Brown. January 2003.

Houston. She had a son, Iain, the same age as Samantha. Laurel would often pick up Samantha and take her along with Iain to the zoo on Saturdays. Laurel and her husband, Jon, were part of our inner circle. She loved gardening and had a carpet of violets at her house. In the weeks and months after the accident, everyone in our class would be given a small pot full of them to care for and remember her by. Most of us kept them on the windowsills in our offices.

Willie McCool, a fellow Navy pilot, and I had crossed paths briefly at Pax River before we were both selected as astronauts. He had been finishing up his tour as a test pilot when I was just starting mine. I remember the first time I saw his name on a list of the new class and thought it had to be the best astronaut name ever.

I didn't know the other crew members nearly as well because they hadn't been in my class. Rick Husband, the commander, a dedicated family man and Air Force pilot; Kalpana Chawla, the first Indian American woman in space and an aerospace engineer; Mike Anderson, an Air Force pilot ready with a smile; and Ilan Ramon, an Israeli fighter pilot who had been chosen to represent his country on this shuttle mission. Ilan was considered a national hero. The crew left behind a total of twelve children.

It was a terrible blow to lose a group of seven people who were all so warm, generous, and kind.

I can honestly say the *Columbia* accident never for a second made me think about quitting. But my colleagues' deaths gave me a renewed sense that my kids could have grown up without a parent, just as the *Columbia* crew's children have done. The shuttle program was suspended until the accident investigation board could come to a conclusion about what had happened, so I didn't have much to do for the next six months.

In August 2003, the *Columbia* Accident Investigation Board submitted its findings. It did not call for the shuttle program to shut down completely, as some had feared. But after the assembly of the International Space Station was complete, the shuttle orbiters would need to be rebuilt from the ground up, which would be so expensive that most likely the shuttle program would be scrapped. I already knew I would miss the space shuttle.

In October 2003, Leslie gave birth to our second child, Charlotte. Her birth shaped up to be even more difficult than Samantha's. When Charlotte was born, she had no heartbeat and wasn't breathing. I'd had a great deal of training and experience dealing with emergencies, but the situation in the operating room was so upsetting I had to leave. My brother and Samantha were in the waiting room, and they told me that I looked as white as a sheet as I came out of the operating room. I sat with them for what seemed like an eternity, until Leslie's doctor came out to tell us that both Leslie and Charlotte were fine now, though it had been touch and go for a while.

Meanwhile, my mission kept getting reshuffled, which brought changes to my crew. Lisa Nowak and Scott Parazynski were moved to other missions, and Rick Mastracchio joined us. Rick had designed many of the emergency procedures we practiced in the simulator, and I knew this would make him an invaluable crew member.

Part of being an astronaut involves having your health monitored more closely than most people's. Every year I had my annual flight physical in February, the month of my birthday. After my physical in 2007, I was told that I had a slightly elevated level of a blood enzyme that can be an indicator of prostate cancer. Because my levels were just a little high, and because I would be unusually young to be diagnosed with this kind of cancer, I decided to wait until after my upcoming mission was over to investigate it further.

STS-118 was a mission to deliver a number of key components to expand the International Space Station. We were also bringing supplies up to the station and carrying science experiments back down. We would be flying the sixth mission after the loss of *Columbia*.

The crew assignments for this flight were now finalized: Scorch, Rick Mastracchio, Barbara Morgan, Dave Williams, Tracy Caldwell, and, late in our training, Alvin Drew.

Barbara Morgan had been an elementary school teacher in Idaho when she was named a finalist for the Teacher in Space program in 1985. When Christa McAuliffe was chosen to teach lessons from space on *Challenger*, Barbara was named her backup. She trained along with Christa and the *Challenger* crew for the entire year, preparing to complete the mission if for some reason Christa wasn't able to. Seeing *Challenger* explode in the sky over Florida with seven good friends aboard was traumatic. But to her credit, Barbara volunteered to go on the national tour that had been planned for Christa after the mission, visiting schools all over the country to talk about the space shuttle and the importance of education. Barbara wanted the schoolchildren to hear from someone who had shared Christa's dream of flying in space and still had faith in the space program. Barbara officially joined the astronaut corps in 1998 and worked in a number of positions. This flight with me, twenty-one years after the *Challenger* disaster, would be her first flight.

Teacher in Space finalist Christa McAuliffe and her backup, Barbara Morgan, train on NASA's KC-135 zero-gravity aircraft, also known as the vomit comet, in January 1986. Twenty-one years after Christa lost her life in the *Challenger* disaster, Barbara finally flew in space as part of my STS-118 shuttle crew.

Dave Williams was a Canadian astronaut who had worked as an ER doctor in his previous life. Tracy Caldwell was flying her first mission. She looked young for her age, so she was treated as a bit of a kid by many of our astronaut colleagues, but she was conscientious, incredibly detail oriented, and serious, but also fun to be around.

Alvin Drew flew helicopters in combat for the Air Force and then went on to become a helicopter test pilot. He didn't seem thrown off by having been assigned to this flight so late.

For me, training to fly as commander was a completely new challenge. I had to learn my own role, as well as make sure everyone knew his or her job. I had to recognize each crew member's strengths and weaknesses and pull us together as a team. And I had to help the rookies learn the ropes. Because we would have three first-time space flyers on our crew (Barb, Tracy, and Alvin), we were one of the least-experienced crews in shuttle history, with only four previous flights among the seven of us.

This time I knew what to expect at launch, so I could enjoy it a little more, even looking out the window a bit. It had been nearly eight years since I last flew into space, and the sheer instantaneous power was still indescribable. We reached orbit safely and, as on my previous mission, successfully got through the arduous job of turning the rocket ship into a spaceship.

Before I went to sleep, I got an email from the lead shuttle flight director telling me that nine pieces of foam had come off the external tank and three had likely struck the thermal protection system on the bottom of the orbiter, similar to what had doomed *Columbia*. But in *Columbia*'s case, the damage was on a more critical part of the wing. NASA didn't think it was a big deal—foam strikes could frequently be harmless—but were just letting me know out of an abundance of caution.

When we approached ISS the next day, we flew the shuttle through a backflip to point the heat shield at the station so the crew could take up-close pictures. The photos showed a possible problem area on a critical part of the shuttle's bottom. The area was big enough that NASA decided to do a special inspection with the laser system after we docked. That inspection revealed a hole, about three inches by three inches, that went all the way through the thermal protection tiles down to the underlying layer.

The ground emailed me photos of the damage. There was a flurry of discussion on the ground about how this damage would

affect our reentry. We didn't have a lot of choices. We could try
to fix the damage on a spacewalk by filling the hole with a special
putty that had never been proven in flight, or take our chances
and land as is. I talked over the options with my crew and we decided that we could fix the damage if we had to, but would trust
the ground crew's advice if they told us we could reenter safely.

Teams of experts on the ground were analyzing the damage
and how the heat of reentry would affect the tiles. They made
a mock-up of the damaged tiles and tested them with extreme
heat, speed, and force. As I learned about the testing they were
doing, I had more and more confidence that the damage would
not present a risk. Some NASA experts disagreed and thought
we should do the repair. I worried we could accidentally make
the hole bigger or create a new hole, and that the material and
procedures for repairing tiles had never even been tried before.

The day we were to return to Earth, we didn't dwell on the risk.
We focused on our jobs getting the shuttle ready. Then we got
suited up, strapped ourselves into our seats, and began the reentry process. As we slammed into the atmosphere and built up
heat, we watched the hot plasma streaming past our windows and
imagined the shuttle's heat shield under fire. We all knew what
could happen if our decision had been wrong.

"Passing through peak heating," Scorch said calmly. This was
the point when *Columbia* had started to break up.

"Understand," I replied.

About twenty seconds later, we had passed the danger.

"Looks like we dodged that bullet," I said. I couldn't help

thinking about our friends we lost on *Columbia*, and I'm sure the rest of my crew was doing the same.

We were now inside the Earth's atmosphere, and as we slowed below the speed of sound, I took over the controls from the autopilot. I was flying the space shuttle for the very first time in Earth's atmosphere and knew I would have only one chance to land.

As we dove seven times steeper than an airliner and descended twenty times faster, I felt the effects of gravity, vertigo, and a visual symptom called nystagmus, where your eyes jerk up and down. When we reached two thousand feet, I tried to put these physical symptoms out of my mind.

At three hundred feet, I told Scorch, "Gear down."

"Gear's down," Scorch said.

From the time the landing gear was lowered until we landed was only about fifteen seconds. We had a pretty heavy crosswind that day, which made all of this more challenging. By the time we came to a stop, I was perfectly in the center of the runway.

Although there was concern about the damage *Endeavour* experienced during liftoff, our landing was picture-perfect. August 2007.

A few months after I returned from STS-118, I was in D.C. to meet
with members of Congress and went out to dinner with Mark's fiancée, Congresswoman Gabrielle Giffords. I'd first met her in Arizona one afternoon a couple of years earlier when I went to pick
up Mark at the airport. Because of their jobs, they'd been having a
long-distance relationship since the year after his divorce in 2004.
She was friendly, warm, and incredibly enthusiastic about her job as
an Arizona state senator. She impressed me so much after our brief
meeting that I joked to Mark that I wondered what she saw in him.

While we were eating, my phone rang, showing the number
for Steve Lindsey, the chief of the Astronaut Office. As the future fiancée of an astronaut, Gabby knew that when the chief
astronaut calls at an unusual hour, you take the call.

"Scott, I'd like to assign you to a long-duration flight, Expedition Twenty-Five and Twenty-Six. You'd be the commander for
Twenty-Six."

I hesitated before speaking. It's always exciting to get a flight
assignment, but spending five or six months on the International
Space Station wasn't exactly what I had been hoping for.

I sighed. "When's the launch date?" I asked.

"October 2010."

"I understand. Let me talk to Leslie and my kids and I'll get
back to you."

Five or six months away from home would be a long time,
especially with Charlotte still so young. But I also knew I would
take any flight assignment I was given. Leslie and the girls agreed

this was an opportunity I couldn't pass up, so I agreed to join the mission.

Among the things I had to do before I could turn my attention to this new assignment was follow up about my health issue. My latest blood test indicated that the problem had gotten worse. I visited Dr. Brian Miles, at Houston's Methodist Hospital, who gave me two options. I could wait six months and have another blood test then and see what it showed. Or I could have a minor but painful surgical test now to find out whether I have cancer right away.

I didn't want to spend the next six months waiting to find out if I had cancer. If I did, I wanted to take care of it as soon as possible. Waiting could jeopardize my chances to fly my next mission.

I had the test, and a few days later, I learned I had a relatively fast-growing strain of cancer. When you are told you have cancer, especially a fast-growing one, your mind immediately runs wild. Is this pain in my arm a sign the cancer has spread? Will I be okay? I think this fear is a normal reaction to have, even for people who have access to top-notch care. I was immediately sent for more tests, and there was no sign the cancer had spread, which did a lot to set my mind at ease.

I called my brother and told him to get himself checked out. Since we were identical twins, we had a nearly identical genetic blueprint and similar risks. When Mark got checked, it turned out he had the same type of cancer.

I had surgery to remove the cancer in November 2007. My recovery took a long time, just as my surgeon had said it would, and it wasn't fun.

Despite the long recovery overall, I worked hard to get my

NASA qualifications back, and I was able to start flying again in January thanks to the skill of Dr. Miles and the NASA flight surgeons. The next year, I was in the operating room while Dr. Miles performed Mark's operation. His tumor was on the opposite side from mine, a mirror image, just like the opposite birthmarks on our foreheads.

11

I BEGAN TRAINING for my mission to the space station in late 2007, with the launch scheduled for October 2010. Missions to ISS were divided into expeditions of six crew members, and my time on station would cover both Expeditions 25 and 26. The mission training took place around the world: at Star City, Russia; at the European Astronaut Centre, in Cologne, Germany; and at the Japanese space agency in Tsukuba, a city of around 200,000 located about fifty miles northeast of Tokyo.

I had a lot of experience working with the Russians in Star City by this point, which would make my training a little easier. I'd already learned that even though my Russian colleagues may seem unfriendly at first, once I got to know them, they'd be warm and affectionate.

While I was focusing on my training all over the world, Leslie continued to take care of things on the home front. I appreciated all she did to be a good mother to Samantha and Charlotte, but I had become more and more unhappy in our marriage. All the time we spent apart didn't help, either.

In the spring of 2009, while I was training in Japan, I had a major personal realization. The weather was gray and dull, I had a bad cold, I was exhausted from jet lag, and I was in a foul mood the whole time. It was then that I realized that despite being miserable in Tsukuba, I would rather be here feeling unhappy than feeling miserable in my own home.

I visited my grandmother the day after I returned to the States. Her home had been such a sanctuary for Mark and me when we were boys. She was now in her nineties, ill and living in a nursing home in Houston. While I sat with her, holding her fragile hand, I thought about where I would be when I was her age, decades in the future. If I were lucky enough to be alive still, what sort of life would I have to look back on? How was I going to spend the rest of my life?

The very next day, I called Leslie from work at the Johnson Space Center and let her know I would be coming home early and that I needed to talk to her alone when I got there. At home, I told her I would always respect her as the mother of our children, and I would always take care of my daughters, but I wanted a divorce. I wish we could have had a happier ending, but I have never regretted my decision to marry her—and I am eternally grateful for Samantha and Charlotte.

Now I had to get my daughters through this difficult time. When they got home from school, I spoke to them as calmly as I could, trying to make things seem positive, though they could tell from their mother's face that they weren't. Samantha was more upset than Charlotte—she was old enough to understand what a big change this was going to be. I tried to assure both of them that I would do everything I could to keep their lives happy and normal.

When I put my head on the pillow that night, I felt more at peace than I had in months, maybe years. I was going to try to live a life I wouldn't regret when I was old.

Missions to the International Space Station lasted approximately six months. As the mission got closer, I trained with my crewmates Sasha Kaleri, the Soyuz commander, and Oleg Skripochka, who would fly in the left seat as the flight engineer. Sasha is a quiet and serious guy with a full head of dark hair speckled with gray. He was one of the most experienced cosmonauts, having flown three long-duration missions on *Mir* and one on the ISS— 608 days altogether. Oleg was on his first spaceflight. Studious and well prepared, he tried to model himself after Sasha in every way, and in turn, Sasha treated Oleg like a son or a little brother.

By now, I was very familiar with the way the Russian space agency handles training. Some things are similar at NASA, such as an emphasis on simulator training. And some things are very different, like their extreme emphasis on the book learning versus hands-on practical experience.

If NASA were to train an astronaut how to mail a package, they would take a box, put an object in the box, show you the route to the post office, and send you on your way with postage. The Russians would start in the forest with a discussion of the species of tree used to create the pulp that will make up the box, then go into excruciating detail on the history of box making. Eventually you would get to the practical information about how the package is actually mailed, if you didn't fall asleep first.

Another uniquely Russian spaceflight practice was the creation of custom-molded seat liners for each crew member. I'd already had my own custom seat made the first time I served as a backup crew member. I was helped into a container like a small bathtub, then had warm plaster poured in all around me. After the plaster hardened, I was helped out, then got to watch while an older technician carved away the excess plaster to create a perfect mold of my back and butt.

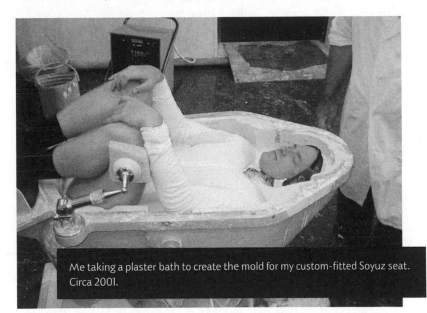

Me taking a plaster bath to create the mold for my custom-fitted Soyuz seat. Circa 2001.

A few weeks later, I came back for a fit check of the newly made seat liner. This was followed by the dreaded pressure check—an hour and a half on my back in my custom-made spacesuit in my custom-made seat liner with the suit pressurized. The circulation in my lower legs got cut off, and the position became a distinctly painful form of torture.

After a few more weeks, I came back for the pressure check again, this time in a vacuum chamber. This is a ritual meant to give us confidence that the suits won't leak in space. These activities can feel more like rituals rather than necessities. This is the case with so many of the traditions in the Russian space program.

In the year between my divorce and my mission launch, I met my wife, Amiko Kauderer. Amiko had been an acquaintance of mine since she had worked at NASA for a long time. She'd worked closely with my brother on a NASA project and also shared mutual friends with my ex-wife, Leslie. In early 2009, Amiko and I both happened to file for divorce at the same time. Then, by coincidence, we ran into each other a few times many months later. We started seeing each other that fall, and things between us had become serious by the time I was leaving for space in October 2010. This would be my first long-duration mission to the International Space Station and her first mission as the partner left behind. It was an unusual challenge for a new relationship.

That morning, our crew went through the full rituals of getting suited up, doing our leak checks, and saying good-bye to our loved ones. We rode the bus out to the launchpad and climbed into the capsule amid a lot of media coverage and fanfare. Among the things we had to do to get the vehicle ready was configure the oxygen system, a task that was my responsibility as the flight engineer 2. Toward the end of the launch countdown, I was turning one of the O_2 valves when we heard a loud squeal. We correctly guessed it was compressed oxygen leaking into the cabin. I immediately closed the valve, but we had a massive oxygen leak anytime the valve was taken out of the closed position. We needed oxygen to breathe during the flight, so keeping the valve closed was not an option.

At the direction of the ground, Sasha tried to get the situation under control by venting the O_2 out through a valve that led to the outside. I looked at the readings on our LCD screens and did some calculations. There was close to 40 percent oxygen in the capsule, which meant that even a small spark could ignite a fire.

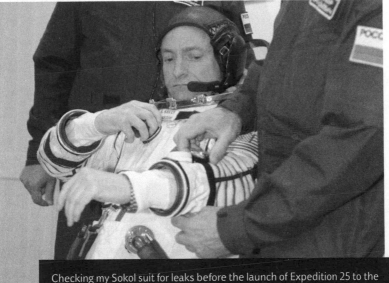

Checking my Sokol suit for leaks before the launch of Expedition 25 to the International Space Station. October 2010.

All astronauts knew that the crew of Apollo 1 had been killed in their capsule because it had been pumped full of pure oxygen and a tiny spark caused a massive fire. NASA didn't use high-pressure oxygen anymore for this reason. They also redesigned all hatches on capsules to open outward. Not the Russians. The hatch on our Soyuz opened inward, so if there was a fire, the outward pressure from the expanding hot gases would force the hatch closed, trapping us, just like the crew of Apollo 1.

I thought, *This is not a good place to be right now.*

"It's too bad we won't launch today," I said.

"*Da,*" Sasha agreed. "We will be first crew to scrub after strapping in since 1969." This is an incredible statistic, considering how often the space shuttle used to scrub, right up to the seconds before launch, even after the main engines had lit.

A voice from the control center interrupted us. "Guys, start your Sokol suit leak checks."

What? Sasha and I looked at each other with identical shocked expressions. We were now inside five minutes to launch. We closed our visors and rushed through the leak check procedures. With less than two minutes to spare, we were ready to go. We settled into our seats for our last minutes on Earth.

The Soyuz launch experience was different from the shuttle— its capsule was much smaller than the space shuttle's cockpit, and the Soyuz in general was less sophisticated, so there was less for the crew to do. Still, it was much more automated than the space shuttle was. Nothing could match the acceleration of the shuttle's solid rocket boosters pushing us away from the Earth with an instantaneous 7 million pounds of thrust at liftoff, but anytime you rocket off the planet, it's serious business.

Once we reached orbit, we were stuck in this cold tin can with very little to do for two whole days until we were to dock with the space station. As the spacecraft moved in and out of communication coverage, the sun rising and setting every ninety minutes, we quickly lost track of any normal sense of time and drifted in and out of sleep. The Soyuz was cramped and spartan. I had brought my iPod, but the battery soon died. I spent most of the time floating in the middle of the module, feeling like I did when I was a kid in after-school detention, staring at the clock, waiting for the day to be over.

Years later, I learned more about what went on that day in the launch center in Baikonur. Someone in launch control had said that they understood this problem, and that there was a workaround: opening the oxygen valve partway, then closing it again before opening it all the way. This worked to unstick the problem valve. In the minutes before launch, officials were passing around a piece of paper they needed to sign indicating that they were go for launch in spite of the oxygen leak and Sasha's struggle to get rid of the extra oxygen as time ticked away. As a crew member getting ready to ride the rocket to space, I found this procedure to be absolutely crazy.

When we finally docked, and I floated through the hatch to officially join the crew of Expedition 25 on the ISS, I was elated to be starting a long-duration mission.

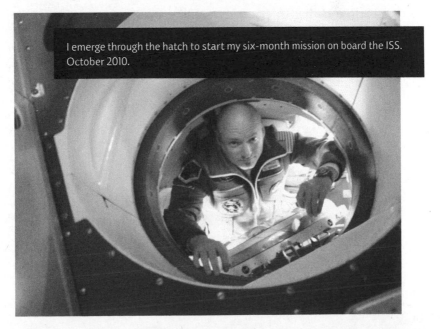

I emerge through the hatch to start my six-month mission on board the ISS. October 2010.

Already on board were two Americans and one Russian. Doug Wheelock was serving as the commander for this expedition and would be turning over command of ISS to me when he left. Doug was a great first ISS commander to serve under. He took a hands-off approach to leadership, letting everyone find his or her own strengths. And we already knew each other from our winter survival training in Russia years ago.

My other American crewmate was Shannon Walker. I didn't know Shannon very well, but I was quickly impressed with her abilities as a crew member.

The Russian cosmonaut Fyodor Yurchikhin was a short, stocky guy with a broad smile. Fyodor was one of only two people I've been in space with more than once (the other being Al Drew). He loved taking pictures of the Earth and showing them to his crewmates no matter what they were trying to do at the time. The cosmonauts aboard ISS generally don't have as busy a schedule as the Americans do, and sometimes they are free to socialize during the day, floating around the dining room table sharing coffee or a snack, while we rush from one assigned task to the next.

On this mission, I learned the differences between visiting space and living there. On a long-duration flight, you work at a slower pace. You get more comfortable moving around, sleep better, digest better. As my first long-duration mission went on, what surprised me most was how little effort it actually took to move around and to hold myself still. With just a slight push of a finger or a toe, I could travel across a module and wind up exactly where I wanted to be.

Lunch break with Doug Wheelock and Shannon Walker. November 7, 2010.

One of my first tasks was repairing a device called Sabatier, an important part of the ecosystem of the station. It must keep the right balance of oxygen and carbon dioxide (CO_2) on board while creating essential water to allow humans to survive in space. My job was to tune the system, a tedious multiday task. Without Shannon's help, the task would have been nearly impossible for me to carry out so early in the mission.

I celebrated my first Thanksgiving on the space station two months later, shortly before taking over as commander of ISS for the first time. The next day, Shannon, Doug, and Fyodor departed for Earth, leaving behind Sasha, Oleg, and me.

After being alone in the American module for a few weeks, the new crew arrived. American astronaut Cady Coleman was a retired colonel in the U.S. Air Force and held a PhD in chemistry and, I came to learn, played the flute. Sometimes I would get up to use the bathroom at three a.m. on a work night and find her playing her flute in the Cupola, a module made entirely of windows looking down on Earth. Cady taught me how to be more in touch with my feelings and those of the people we worked with on the ground. She also helped me see the value of letting the public share the excitement of what we were doing in space. This would turn out to be enormously helpful on my yearlong mission.

The Italian astronaut Paolo Nespoli, a talented engineer with a great sense of humor, was the third member of the new crew. Paolo is really tall—too tall to fit into the Soyuz, in fact. The European Space Agency had to pay the Russians more money to modify the seat, setting it at a steeper angle, in order to fit him into the capsule.

The new Soyuz commander was Dima Kondratyev, my survival training buddy. This was his first spaceflight.

January 8, 2011, was a bright sunny day in Tucson, Arizona, but on the space station, the weather was the same as always, and I was fixing a toilet. I had taken it apart and organized the pieces around me so they wouldn't float away, and now I would not do anything else until I finished the job. The toilet is one of the pieces of equipment that gets a great deal of our attention—if both toilets break, we could use the Soyuz toilet, but it wouldn't last long. Then we would have to abandon ship. If we were on our way to Mars and the toilet broke and we couldn't fix it, we would be dead.

I was so involved in the work that I didn't notice the TV feed being cut. We lost our signal pretty routinely, so I didn't think it was a big deal. Then a call came from the ground.

Mission control told me that Peggy Whitson, now the chief of the Astronaut Office, needed to talk to me and would be calling on a private line in five minutes. I had no idea why, but I knew the reason couldn't be anything good.

Five minutes is a long time to think about what emergency might have occurred on the ground. Maybe my grandmother had died. Maybe one of my daughters had been hurt. I didn't make any connection between the blank TV screen and the phone call—NASA had deliberately cut the feed to keep me from learning bad news.

Peggy came on the line. "I don't know how to tell you this," she said, "so I'm just going to tell you. Your sister-in-law, Gabby, was shot."

I was stunned. This was such a shocking thing to hear, it seemed surreal. Peggy said she didn't have any more information, and I told her I wanted to know any news as it came in, that she shouldn't keep secrets to spare me. Even if the information was unconfirmed or incomplete, I still wanted to know.

When I got off the line, I told the crew what had happened and tried to assure everyone I was going to be okay. But I also told them I was going to need some time and that I was going to spend most of it on the phone. They were shocked and upset as well and of course gave me the room I needed. Though I was hesitant to turn over this crucial job of fixing the toilet to Cady and Paolo, I had no choice but to trust them.

I liked Gabby from the first time I met her, and I've only gotten to like her more over the years. She treats everyone the same—she is interested in everyone she meets, no matter who they are, where they are from, or what political party they vote for. She wants to help everyone she comes across, and she was completely dedicated to her work as a congresswoman on behalf of the people of Arizona. That was why it was so hard to understand what had occurred. This sort of random violence should never happen to anyone, but it seemed especially awful that this should happen to her. As astronauts, Mark and I had been confronted with the risks of flying in space. None of us could have imagined that it would be Gabby, not Mark, whose work nearly cost her her life.

I called Mark. He was frantically packing his bags in Houston as we talked and had arranged to fly to Tucson as quickly as possible. He told me he'd been awakened by a call from Pia Carusone, Gabby's chief of staff, telling him about the shooting. Pia told him that Gabby had been shot at a public event, that an unknown number of people had been hurt or killed, that Gabby's condition was uncertain, and that he needed to get to Tucson right away.

Mark and I agreed we would connect again as soon as he landed in Tucson. Not long after, mission control called to tell me that the Associated Press was reporting that Gabby had died. The next several hours were some of the longest in my life. My mind kept traveling to my brother—what he must be feeling, not knowing whether he would ever see his wife alive again. When Mark landed in Arizona, he called me.

"What's happening?" I asked the moment I picked up. "They're saying Gabby died."

"I know," he said. "I got the news on the plane. But I just spoke to the hospital, and it was a mistake. She's still alive."

There is no way to describe the relief you feel when you've been told someone you care about is alive after spending hours thinking she was dead. We knew Gabby would still have a long and hard road ahead of her, but knowing she was still drawing breath was the best news we could have hoped for.

I made dozens more calls that day and the next—to my brother, to Amiko, to my mother and father, to my daughters, to friends. That first day, I learned that thirteen other people had been injured in the shooting and six had been killed, including a nine-year-old girl named Christina-Taylor Green, who was interested in politics and had wanted to meet Gabby.

On Monday, President Obama announced a national day of mourning. On the space station, we followed our normal routine. But I knew that on Earth some things would never be the same.

My brother had been assigned to the second-to-last flight of the space shuttle program, a mission to deliver components to the International Space Station. He was scheduled to fly on April 1, less than three months after the shooting. Gabby's condition was stable, but she had a long road of surgeries and therapy ahead of her. He wanted to be there for Gabby as she started the long process of recovering, but he also felt a duty to see his mission through. He and his crewmates had been training together for months, and a new commander would not know the mission or the crew as well as Mark did. We talked on the phone about it many times, but in the end, it was Gabby who made the decision. She would have been devastated if the shooting had robbed him of his last chance to fly in space. She urged him to go.

In February, *Discovery*—the shuttle I had flown on my first flight—came up and docked with the station on its last flight. It was funny seeing a shuttle crew come on board, as I had done myself not that long before, flying around in the Superman position—floating horizontally—rather than the more upright position of seasoned long-term space travelers. The new guys were bumping into everything and kicking equipment off the walls everywhere they went.

Shortly after *Discovery* and its crew returned to Earth, it would have its engines removed and would be sent to the Smithsonian's National Air and Space Museum in Washington, D.C., to become a permanent display. *Discovery* had left Earth more times than any spacecraft in history, a record of distinction that I expect it to keep for a long time to come.

Sasha, Oleg, and I were scheduled to return to Earth on March 16, 2011. Having never experienced reentry on the Soyuz, I was curious what it would be like. I had been given a range of different impressions by different people—that it would be terrifying, that it would be fine, and that it would actually be fun, like Mr. Toad's Wild Ride at Disney World.

That day everyone was concerned about the weather, because there were blizzard conditions at the landing site. Our capsule smacked into the hard frozen surface of the desert steppes of Kazakhstan, bounced around, tipped over, then was dragged a hundred yards by the parachute. I've never been in a car accident that ended in multiple rollovers, but I imagine that landing in the Soyuz that day felt a lot like that—violently jarring. But I found it exhilarating and I knew with certainty that I would long to do it over and over again.

Me after my Soyuz landing in March 2011, wearing an I ♥ GABBY bracelet in support of my sister-in-law, Gabby Giffords, who had been shot during my mission.

Eventually, the rescue forces collected the parachute and knocked it down before it could drag us any farther. Not long after, the hatch opened and the blizzard blew into the capsule—the first fresh air I had smelled in six months. It was incredibly refreshing, a sensation I'll never forget.

When I returned to Earth, Amiko and I were both surprised to find that the separation had only brought us closer. I had been able to depend on her as my partner on the ground, and we enjoyed being able to give each other our undivided attention for the hour or so a day we could talk on the phone. I came back more confident than ever that we belonged together. A few days later, when we got back to the U.S., Amiko and I went to visit Gabby at TIRR Memorial Hermann, the rehab hospital where she was being treated. I was shocked at first by how different she looked. She was in a wheelchair and was wearing a helmet to protect her head where a piece of her skull had been removed to give her brain more room to swell. Her hair was short—it had been shaved for brain surgery—and her face looked different. It took me a moment to process the enormity of what had happened to her. When I heard she had been shot, I had understood intellectually what that meant. But it was another thing entirely to see my vivacious sister-in-law in such a different state—not only physically changed but unable to speak as she once had. Sometimes Gabby would get a look on her face as if she had something to say, and when we all looked at her and paused, she would say, simply, "Chicken." Then she'd roll her eyes at herself—that wasn't what she wanted to say!—and try again.

"Chicken."

I could see how frustrating it was for Gabby, who used to make speeches to thousands of people that inspired them and won their votes. Mark explained that the gunshot to her brain caused aphasia, a disorder that made it hard for her to speak, though her ability to understand language, her intelligence, and, most important, her personality remained unaffected. She understood everything we said to her, but putting her own thoughts into words was extremely hard. We had dinner together at the hospital, and as the visit went on, I could see Gabby's warmth and her sense of humor.

Less than two months later, I was standing next to Gabby on the roof of the Launch Control Center at Cape Canaveral, watching *Endeavour* prepare to launch for its last mission, with Mark as its commander. When Mark had decided he would see this mission through, Gabby had set the goal of being well enough to fly to Florida and be here to see him off. That had been extremely ambitious, and she had done it. For Gabby, just being here to support Mark was an accomplishment on par with a shuttle launch. She seemed to thrive on the challenge to do hard things.

Soon after Mark's mission, the space shuttle was retired, as decided by the *Columbia* Accident Investigation Board. I was sad to see it go. It was the spacecraft I'd learned to fly and learned to love, and I doubt we'll see anything like it again in my lifetime.

In 2012, NASA learned the Russians were going to send a cosmonaut to the space station for a year. Once this had been announced, it put NASA in the position of having to either explain why an American astronaut was not up to the same challenge or announcing a yearlong mission themselves. To their credit, they chose the latter.

Once the Year in Space mission had been announced, NASA still had to choose the astronaut to do it. At first, I wasn't sure I wanted it to be me. I remembered exactly how long 159 days on the space station had felt. Spending twice as long up there wouldn't just feel twice as long, I thought—it could seem much longer. I knew I would miss Amiko and my daughters and my life on Earth.

But I had decided a long time before always to say yes to whatever challenge came my way. This yearlong mission was the hardest thing I'd ever have the opportunity to do, and I decided I wanted to be the one to do it.

Many other astronauts also expressed interest. After all, spaceflight opportunities don't come around every day. The requirements to be considered were many: we had to have previously flown a long-duration flight, we had to be certified to do spacewalks, we had to be capable of being assigned as commander, we had to be medically qualified, and we had to be available to be off the Earth for that year. Only two people had experience that checked every box: Jeff Williams, one of my astronaut classmates, and me.

A few weeks later, I learned I would be flying in space for a year.

When I was preparing for the press conference to announce Misha and me as the one-year crew members, I asked what I thought was an innocent question about genetic research. I mentioned something we hadn't previously discussed: Mark being on the ground with the same DNA as me would be a perfect way to study the actual impact of space on my body throughout the year. The Twins Study became an important aspect of the research being done on station. A lot of people have assumed that I was chosen for this mission because I have an identical twin, but that was actually a lucky bonus.

The yearlong mission was announced in November 2012, with cosmonaut Mikhail Kornienko and me as the crew. The idea of leaving the Earth for a year didn't feel especially real until a couple of months before I was to go. On January 20, 2015, I attended the State of the Union address at the invitation of President Obama. It was an honor to sit in the House Chamber with the gathered members of Congress, the Joint Chiefs, the cabinet secretaries, and the Supreme Court. I sat in the gallery wearing my bright blue NASA flight jacket over a shirt and tie. The president described the goals of the yearlong mission—to solve the problems of getting to Mars—and called me out personally.

"Good luck, Captain!" he said. "Make sure to Instagram it! We're proud of you."

The entire Congress got to their feet and applauded. I stood and gave an awkward nod and a wave. To see the government come together, even if only in a physical sense, was touching, and it was great to experience in person the complete support NASA often enjoys.

I was seated next to Alan Gross, who had been held in a

Cuban prison for five years. He suggested that while I was in space I should count up—count the number of days I had been there—rather than counting down the number of days I had left. It will be easier that way, he said. And that's exactly what I did.

Me being honored by President Obama at the State of the Union address in Washington, D.C., before my Year in Space mission. January 20, 2015.

PART 3

MY YEAR IN SPACE

The flags of Kazakhstan, Russia, the United States, and the Russian Federal Space Agency welcome Mikhail Kornienko, Gennady Padalka, and me to the Baikonur Cosmodrome, as we prepare to launch to the ISS.

12

YOU HAVE TO go to the ends of the Earth in order to leave the Earth. Since the space shuttles were retired in 2011, we've depended on the Russians to launch us into space, and we must start with a journey to the Baikonur Cosmodrome on the desert steppes of Kazakhstan. In February, I fly from Houston to Moscow, a familiar journey of eleven hours. From there I ride in a van to Star City, Russia, 45 miles away. From Star City, we fly 1,600 miles to Baikonur, once the secret launch site for the Soviet space program. People sometimes say that a place is "in the middle of nowhere," but I never say that anymore unless I'm talking about Baikonur. It's a desolate and brutal place, and it's the only working human spaceport for most of the world.

I'm descending toward Baikonur in a Tupolev 134, an old Russian military transport plane with an international crew of space travelers—Russian, American, European, Japanese, and Canadian. We are former enemies remade as crewmates, on our way to the space station we built together.

When we land on Baikonur's single runway, we are greeted by a welcoming party that includes the mayor of Baikonur and other local dignitaries. My Russian crewmate Gennady Padalka strides forward and speaks sternly to them as we stand at semi-attention: *"My gotovy k sleduyushchim shagam nashey podgotovki."* ("We are ready for the next steps of our preparation.")

Our Expedition 43 crew welcoming ceremony in Baikonur, Kazakhstan. From left to right: me, Gennady Padalka, and Mikhail Kornienko. March 14, 2015.

This is a ritual, like so many in spaceflight. We Americans have similar staged moments at similar points of launch preparation. There is a fine line between ritual and superstition, and in a life-threatening business such as spaceflight, superstition can be comforting even to the nonbeliever.

We see a strange but welcoming sight at the edge of the tarmac: a group of Kazakh kids holding balloons, little ambassadors from the end of the Earth. The Russian flight doctor has warned us to stay away from them: there has been a measles outbreak in this region, and if one of us were to be infected, it would bring serious consequences. We have all been vaccinated, but the Russian flight surgeons are very cautious. Normally we do what the doctor says, especially since he has the power to ground us. But Gennady walks confidently forward anyway.

"We must say hello to the children," he says firmly in English.

I've known both Gennady and Misha since the late 1990s. Gennady is fifty-six and is the commander of our Soyuz. He's a natural leader and I trust him completely. Once, in Moscow, near the Kremlin, I saw him break away from his fellow cosmonauts to pay his respects at the site where an anti-government politician had been murdered. For a cosmonaut, an employee of Putin's government, that gesture was risky.

Misha, my fellow traveler for a year, is fifty-four and is very different from Gennady. He is the most laid-back Russian I have ever met, quiet and thoughtful. Misha's father was a military helicopter pilot for the cosmonaut rescue forces and died when Misha was only five in a helicopter crash. This personal tragedy only made him want to fly more. He was selected as a cosmonaut in 1998.

When Misha stares at you with his light blue eyes, it feels like nothing is more important to him than fully understanding what you are saying. He is more open with his feelings than the other Russians I know.

After we greet the Kazakh kids, everyone boards two buses for the ride to the quarantine facility where we will spend the next two weeks. (The prime crew and backup crew always travel separately, just in case something happens to one of us.)

We pass dilapidated Soviet-era apartment complexes, huge rusted satellite dishes still communicating with Russian spacecraft, mounds of garbage randomly strewn about, the occasional camel. It's a clear, sunny day. We pass Baikonur's own statue of Yuri Gagarin.

Gennady, Misha, and me in front of a second statue Yuri Gagarin, this time in a triumphant pose, in Baikonur. March 2015.

Far over the horizon a launch tower rises above the same deteriorating concrete pad from which Yuri first rocketed off Earth, the same pad from which nearly every Russian cosmonaut has left Earth, the same pad from which I will leave Earth two weeks from now. The Russians sometimes seem to care more about tradition than they do about appearance or function.

Misha's and my mission to spend a year on ISS is unprecedented. A normal mission to the space station lasts five to six months, so scientists have a good deal of data about what happens to the human body in space for that length of time. But very little is known about what happens after month six. The symptoms might get suddenly worse in the ninth month, for instance, or they might level off. We don't know, and there is only one way to find out.

Misha and I will collect various types of data for studies on our bodies, which will take a significant amount of our time. This is in addition to the Twin Study. The International Space Station is a world-class orbiting laboratory, and I will spend a lot of my time this year working on other experiments.

Since she wasn't able to travel to Baikonur for my Year in Space launch, my sister-in-law, Gabby, visits mission control at the Johnson Space Center. Left to right: Johnson Space Center director Ellen Ochoa, Gabby, and astronaut Mike Fossum. March 2015.

Looking out the window at the strange landscape of Baikonur, I realize that for all the time I've spent here, weeks in fact, I have never really seen the town itself. I've only been to the designated spaces where I have official business: the hangars where the engineers and technicians prepare our spacecraft and rocket for flight; the windowless fluorescent-lit rooms where we get into our Sokol pressure suits; the building where our instructors, interpreters, doctors, cooks, management people, and other support staff stay; and the nearby building, affectionately called Saddam's Palace by Americans, where we stay. This opulent residence was built for the head of the Russian space agency and his staff and guests, and he allows the crew to use it while we're here. Saddam's Palace has crystal chandeliers, marble floors, and a four-room suite for each of us, complete with Jacuzzi tubs. The building also has a *banya*, or Russian sauna, with a cold pool to jump into afterward.

We all gather in the elaborate dining room for meals served on pressed white tablecloths and fine china, with a flat-screen TV on the wall that constantly plays old Russian movies the cosmonauts seem to love. The Russian food is good, but for Americans, it can start to get old after a while—borscht (a traditional soup made from beets) at nearly every meal, meat and potatoes, other kinds of meat and potatoes, everything covered with tons of dill.

"Gennady," I say while we are eating dinner. "What's with all the dill?"

"What do you mean?" he asks.

"You guys put dill on everything. Some of this food might actually be good if it weren't covered in dill."

"Ah, okay, I understand," Gennady says, nodding, his signature smile starting to emerge. "It's from when the Russian diet consisted mostly of potatoes, cabbage, and vodka. Dill gets rid of farts."

Later I Google it and it's true. As it happens, getting rid of gas is a worthwhile goal before being sealed into a small tin can together for many hours, so I stop complaining about the dill.

The day after we arrive in Baikonur we have the first "fit check." This is our opportunity to get inside the Soyuz capsule while it's still in the hangar. In the cavernous hangar known as Building 254, we pull on our Sokol suits—always an awkward process. The only way into the suits is through the opening in the chest, so we have to slide our lower bodies into the chest hole, then struggle to fit our arms into the sleeves while blindly pulling the neck ring up over our heads. The chest opening is then gathered together and secured using very low-tech elastic bands. The first time I saw this, I couldn't believe those elastic bands were all that protected us from space. Once I got to the ISS, I learned the Russians use the exact same elastic bands to seal their garbage bags in space. In one sense I find this comical; in another way, I respect the efficiency of the Russian philosophy on technology. If it works, why change it?

The Sokol suit was designed as a rescue suit, which means that its only function is to save us in case of a fire or depressurization in the Soyuz. It's different from the spacesuit I will wear during spacewalks. That suit will be a little spaceship in its own right. The Sokol suit serves the same purpose as the orange NASA-designed pressure suit worn to fly the space shuttle after the *Challenger* disaster of 1986. Before that, shuttle astronauts wore simple cloth flight suits, as the Russians did before a depressurization accident killed three cosmonauts in 1971. Since then, cosmonauts (and any astronauts to join them in the Soyuz) have worn the Sokol suits. In a weird way, we are surrounded by the evidence of tragedies, too-late fixes that might have saved the astronauts and cosmonauts who took the same risks we are taking and lost.

Today is like a dress rehearsal: we suit up, perform leak checks, then get strapped into our custom-made seats, built from the plaster molds taken of our bodies.

As much time as I have spent in the Soyuz simulators in Star City, I'm still amazed by how difficult it is to wedge myself and my Sokol suit into my seat. Each time, I have a moment of doubt whether I'm going to fit. But then I do—just barely. I wonder how my taller colleagues do it. Once we're strapped in, we practice reaching out for buttons, reading data off screens, grabbing our checklists. We discuss where we want our timers (used for timing engine burns), where we want our pencils, and where we want the bits of Velcro that will allow us to put things "down" in space.

When we finish, we clamber back out of the hatch and look around the dusty hangar. The next Progress resupply rocket is here; it looks very similar to the Soyuz, because the Russians never create two designs when one will do. In a few months, this Progress will deliver equipment, experiments, food, oxygen, and care packages to us on the ISS. After that, another Soyuz will launch in July carrying a new three-person crew. Somewhere in this hangar, the parts for the next Soyuz to fly after that are being assembled, and another one after that, and another one after that. The Russians have been launching the Soyuz since I was three years old.

The Soyuz spacecraft—Soyuz means "union," as in "Soviet Union," in Russian—is designed to maneuver in space, dock with the station, and keep human beings alive. The rockets (which for some odd reason are also called Soyuz) are prepared for launch in an assembly and test facility across from the hangars known as site 112. Gennady, Misha, and I cross the street, pass the gathered Russian media, and enter that enormous building to look at our rocket. Gunmetal gray, it lies on its side. Unlike the space shuttle or the colossal Apollo/Saturn that came before it, the Soyuz spacecraft and rocket combination is assembled on its side and rolled out to the launchpad in that position. Only when it reaches the launchpad, a couple of days before we launch, will it be stood upright, pointing toward its destination.

Our Soyuz TMA-16M spacecraft rolls out by train to the historic launchpad at the Baikonur Cosmodrome. March 2015.

At 162 feet long, this rocket, the Soyuz-FG, is noticeably smaller than the space shuttle, but it's still a daunting colossus, a building-size object that will, we hope, leave the ground, with us riding on top of it, at twenty-five times the speed of sound. The Soyuz-FG is the grandchild of the Soviet R-7, the world's first intercontinental ballistic missile. The R-7 was designed during the Cold War for launching nuclear weapons at American targets. I can't help remembering how as a child I was aware that New York City, and my suburb of West Orange, New Jersey, would certainly have been among the first targets to be instantly vaporized by a Soviet attack. Today, I'm standing inside their formerly secret facility, discussing with two Russians our plans to trust one another with our lives while riding to space on this converted weapon.

Gennady, Misha, and I all served in our militaries before being chosen to fly in space, and though it's something we never talk about, we all know we could have been ordered to kill one another.

Now we are taking part in the largest peaceful international collaboration in history. When people ask whether the space station is worth the expense, this is something I always point out. What is it worth to see former bitter enemies transform their weapons into transport for peaceful exploration and the pursuit of scientific knowledge? What is it worth to see former enemy nations turn their warriors into crewmates and lifelong friends? This is impossible to put a dollar figure on, but to me it's one of the things that make this project worth the expense, even worth risking our lives.

The International Space Station got its start in 1984, when President Ronald Reagan announced during his State of the Union address that NASA was designing a space station, *Freedom,* to be put in orbit within ten years. Resistance from Congress created years of cutbacks, and *Freedom* was no closer to actually being built when, in 1993, President Clinton announced that the station would be merged with the Russian Federal Space Agency's proposed space station *Mir-2.* With the addition of space agencies representing Europe, Japan, and Canada, the international coalition came to include fifteen countries. It took more than one hundred launches to get the components into orbit and more than one hundred spacewalks to assemble them. The ISS is a remarkable achievement of technology and international cooperation. It has been inhabited nonstop since November 2, 2000. Put another way, it has been more than eighteen years since all humans were on the Earth at once. It is by far the longest-inhabited structure in space and has been visited by more than two hundred people from sixteen nations. So it is especially fitting that Misha and I would spend this record-breaking year together, representing both of our countries.

I wake up on March 27, my last morning on Earth, at around seven. My last earthly breakfast is a Baikonur attempt at American cuisine: runny eggs, toast, and "breakfast sausages" (actually microwaved hot dogs). Getting ready on the day of launch takes much longer than you'd think it would, like so many aspects of spaceflight. I savor a bath in the Jacuzzi tub, then a nap (because our launch is scheduled for 1:42 a.m. local time). When I wake, I take a shower, lingering awhile. I know how much I'll miss the feeling of water for the next year.

The Russian flight surgeon we call "Dr. No" shows up shortly after I'm out of the shower. He is called Dr. No because he gets to decide whether our families can see us once we're in quarantine. He is here to wipe down our entire bodies with alcohol wipes to kill any germs trying to stow away with space travelers. That's followed by a champagne toast with senior management and our significant others; then we sit in silence for a minute, a Russian tradition before a long trip. As we leave the building, a Russian Orthodox priest will bless us and throw holy water into each of our faces. Every cosmonaut since Yuri Gagarin has gone through each of these steps, so we will go through them, too. I'm not religious, but I always say that when you're getting ready to be rocketed into space, a blessing can't hurt.

We do a ceremonial walkout past the media and get on the bus that will take us to the building where we get suited up. The moment the door to the bus closes behind us, a rope holding back the crowd is cut, and everyone rushes forward. It's chaotic, and

I can't spot my family at first, but then I see them in the front row—Amiko, Samantha, Charlotte, and Mark. Someone lifts up Charlotte, who is eleven, so she can put her hand on the window, and I put my hand up to hers. Charlotte is smiling, her round white face beaming. If she's sad that she won't see me for a year, if she's scared to watch me leave Earth on a barely controlled bomb, if she's aware of the many types of peril I will face before I get to hug her again a year from now, she doesn't show it. Then she's down on the asphalt again, standing with the rest of them and waving. I see Amiko smiling, though I can also see tears in her eyes. I see Samantha, who is twenty. Her wide smile betrays her apprehension for what is to come.

I sit on a cheap leather couch waiting to suit up in Building 254, a thirty-minute drive from Saddam's Palace. There is some food laid out—cold chicken, meat pies, juice, and tea—and though it isn't what I would have chosen as my final meal made from fresh ingredients for a year, I eat a bit.

We each take our turn in the next room, stripping down and diapering up, cardiac electrodes, and a fresh pair of white long underwear (meant to absorb sweat and shield us from the rubber of the Sokol suit). It's now time to get our Sokol suits on. We have white-coated, surgical-masked Russian specialists to help us get dressed. They expertly close the openings in our suits with a series of folds and the peculiar rubber bands.

The three of us walk into another nearby room, which is divided by a sheet of glass. On the other side are our families, managers from Roscosmos, NASA leaders, and members of the media sitting in rows of seats facing us. This moment has always made me feel like a gorilla in the zoo.

We talk to the media from behind glass to maintain our quarantine right before the launch for our Year in Space mission as our families look on. March 27, 2015.

I immediately spot Amiko, Mark, and my daughters in the crowd. Amiko and the girls have been here for a few days, but Mark only just arrived. They all smile at me and wave. Not for the first time, I'm grateful that my brother is there for them.

Sitting next to Amiko is Samantha. I'd been surprised to see her new look when she showed up in Baikonur, her long curls dyed black, thick black eyeliner, and dark red lipstick. When I look at her today through the glass, her blue eyes sparkling under the heavy eyeliner, I still see her the way she looked when she was born. When I first saw her tiny pink face with one eye shut and the other eye open, I felt an unbelievable urge to protect her. Though she's an adult now, I still feel the same way.

Charlotte was born when Samantha was almost nine, an age gap that has made it easy for them to get along. Samantha seems to enjoy having an adoring sidekick, and Charlotte has had the freedom to go anywhere her older sister is willing to take her—including to Baikonur. She has grown up to be healthy, bright, strong, and a generous-spirited person. I know she must be experiencing extremes of emotion today, but she seems happy and calm, sitting next to her sister and brushing her light brown bangs out of her eyes to smile at me. I feel grateful that my daughters are able to lean on Amiko for reassurance and to follow her lead in how to deal with the stresses of this week.

On our side of the glass is a mock-up of the Soyuz seat, and one by one, Gennady, Misha, and I get into it, lying on our backs. Technicians check our suits for leaks. I lie there for fifteen minutes with my helmet closed and my knees pressed up to my chest while a large room full of people, some of whom I don't know, watch politely. Why we need to do this for an audience I've never been sure—another ritual. Afterward we sit in a row of chairs before the glass to have a last talk, through microphones, with our families.

My family watches from the other side of the glass as I get ready to head to the launchpad. Left to right: Amiko, Samantha, Charlotte, and Mark. March 27, 2015.

The things we want to say to our loved ones before we might be about to die in a fireball above Kazakhstan are not the things we would want to say while the assembled press from a number of countries listen from rows of chairs and write down our every word. Still, I wouldn't want my daughters' last image to be of me speaking a few terse words into a microphone, so I try to split the difference by saying little but trying to communicate much in other ways, figuring that simple gestures can say a lot. I give Amiko and the girls the "I've got my eyes on you" gesture, pointing back and forth from my eyes to their eyes. It makes them smile.

When we finish this ritual and go outside, it's dark and freezing cold. Floodlights blind us as we walk into the parking lot, flanked by rows of media and spectators we can barely make out.

The bus taking us to the launchpad is waiting nearby. The three of us walk up to three small white squares that have been painted on the asphalt, labeled with our positions on the Soyuz: COMMANDER for Gennady, FLIGHT ENGINEER for Misha, FLIGHT ENGINEER 2 for me. We step into our little boxes and wait for the head of the Russian space agency to ask us each in turn, again, if we are ready for our flight. It's sort of like getting married, except whenever you're asked a question you say, "We are ready for the flight," instead of "I do."

We board the bus—the prime crew, our flight surgeons, the Gagarin Cosmonaut Training Center managers, and a few suit technicians. We sit on the side facing all the lights and clamoring people. I catch sight of my family one last time and give them a wave. The bus slowly pulls away, and they are gone.

Soon, the bus comes to a stop well before the launchpad. We nod at one another, step off, and take up our positions. We've all undone the rubber-band seals that had been so carefully and publicly leak-checked just an hour before. I don't really have to pee, but it's a tradition: When Yuri Gagarin was on his way to the launchpad for his historic first spaceflight, he asked to pull over—right about here—and peed on the right rear tire of the bus. Then he went to space and came back alive. So now we all must do the same. The tradition is so well respected that women space travelers bring a bottle of urine or water to splash on the tire rather than getting entirely out of their suits.

This ritual satisfactorily observed, we get back into the bus, seal back up, and resume the last leg of our journey. A few minutes later, the bus makes another stop to let the train pass that has just fueled our rocket. The bus door opens and an unexpected face appears: my brother's.

This is a breach of quarantine: my brother, having been on a series of germ-infested planes from the United States to Moscow to Baikonur just yesterday, could be carrying all manner of terrible illnesses. Dr. No has been saying "Nyet" all week, and now, suddenly, he sees my brother and says "Da." The Russians enforce the quarantine with an iron fist, then let my brother break it for sentimental reasons; they make a ritual of sealing up our suits, then let us open them to pee on a tire. At times, their inconsistencies drive me nuts, but this gesture, letting me see my brother again when I least expect to, means the world to me. Mark and I don't exchange many words as we ride together for the few minutes out to the launchpad. Here we are, two boys from blue-collar New Jersey who somehow made it such a long way from home.

13

I'M CRAMMED IN the right-hand seat of the Soyuz, acutely aware of the 280 tons of explosive propellant under me. In an hour, we will tear into the sky. For now, soft rock playing over the communication system is distracting us from the pain of sitting in the cramped capsule.

When we got off the bus at the launch site, it was fully dark, floodlights illuminating the launch vehicle so it could be seen from miles around. Though I've done it three times before, approaching the rocket I was about to climb into is still an unforgettable experience. As always, the number of people around the launchpad surprised me, considering how dangerous it is to have a fully fueled rocket—basically a bomb—sitting there. At the Kennedy Space Center, the area was always cleared of nonessential personnel for three miles around, and even the closeout crew drove to a safe viewing site after strapping us into our seats. Today, dozens of people were milling around, some of them smoking, and a few of them will watch the launch from dangerously close.

In 1960, an explosion on the launchpad killed hundreds of people. The Soviets pretended it hadn't happened and sent Yuri Gagarin to space the following year. The Soviet Union acknowledged the disaster only after the information about it was declassified in 1989.

By tradition, there is one last ritual: Gennady, Misha, and I climbed the first few stairs heading toward the elevator, then turned to say good-bye to the assembled crowd, waving to the people of Earth one last time.

Now we wait in the Soyuz, something we've all experienced before, so we know our roles and know what to expect. I anticipate the excruciating pain in my knees that nothing seems to alleviate. I try to distract myself with work and just go down my checklist. The capsule heats up as we wait.

Russian mission control warns us it's one minute to launch. On an American spacecraft, we would already know because we'd see the countdown clock ticking backward toward zero. Unlike NASA, the Russians don't feel the drama of the countdown is necessary. On the space shuttle, I never knew whether I was really going to space that day until I felt the solid rocket boosters light under me; there were always more scrubs than launches. On Soyuz, there is no question. The Russians haven't scrubbed a launch after the crew was strapped in since 1969.

"*My gotovy,*" Gennady responds into his headset. We are ready.

"*Zazhiganiye,*" mission control says. Ignition.

The twenty rocket engines of the first stage roar to full capacity. We sit rumbling on the launchpad for a few seconds, vibrating with the engines' power—we need to burn off some of the fuel to become light enough to lift off. Then our seats push hard into our backs. Some astronauts use the term "kick in the pants" to describe this moment. The slam of acceleration—going from still to the speed of sound in a minute—is heart pounding and addictive, and there is no question that we are going straight up.

Inside, the capsule is dark and loud and we are sweaty in

Misha, Gennady, and me as we pose for the traditional final good-bye to the people of Earth before entering the Soyuz for the launch of Expedition 43. March 27, 2015.

our Sokol suits. My visor fogs up, and I have trouble reading my checklist.

The four strap-on boosters of four engines each fall away smoothly after two minutes, leaving the four remaining engines of the second stage to push us into space. As we accelerate to three times the Earth's gravity, the crushing force smashes me into my seat and makes it difficult to breathe.

Gennady reports to the control center that we are all feeling fine and reads off data from the monitor. My knees hurt, but the excitement of launch has masked the pain some. The second-stage rockets fire for three minutes, and we are feeling their thrust.

Suddenly, we are thrown forward against our straps, then slammed back into our seats. The violence of the second stage has finished, and the third stage has taken over. We feel some roll oscillations in the third stage, a mild sensation of rocking back and forth, which isn't alarming. Then the last engine cuts off with a bang and there is a jolt, like a minor car crash. Then nothing.

Our zero-g talisman, a stuffed snowman belonging to Gennady's youngest daughter, floats on a string. We are in weightlessness as we reach MECO. It's always a shock. The spacecraft is now in orbit around the Earth. After having been subjected to such strong and strange forces, the sudden quiet and stillness feel unnatural.

We smile at one another and reach up for a three-handed high five, happy to have survived this far. We won't feel the weight of gravity again for a very long time.

The Soyuz solar arrays unfurl themselves, and the antennas are deployed. We are now a fully functional spacecraft in orbit. It's a relief, but only briefly.

We open our helmets. The fan noise and pump noise blend-

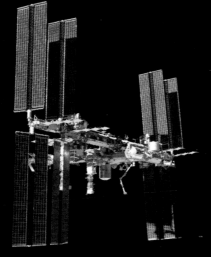

The International Space Station (ISS) with its giant solar arrays appearing to cut through the blackness of space as the moon beckons in the background.

The ISS seen with Earth below.

Mark (left) and me in our yard on Mitchell Street, West Orange, New Jersey. Circa 1967.

Me (left), my father (center), and Mark (right). Circa 1980.

My Radar Intercept Officer (RIO), Bill "Smoke" Mnich, and me flying an F-14 Tomcat in 1995. My years as a test pilot came before my years as an astronaut.

Me about to get a ride on a Navy airplane during one of my summer navy cruises. Circa 1985.

My space shuttle *Discovery* crew, headed to the launchpad for my first spaceflight. From left to right and front to back: me, Curt Brown, John Grunsfeld, Jean-Francois Clervoy (France), Mike Foale, Claude Nicollier (Switzerland), and Steve Smith. December 19, 1999.

Lifting off in *Discovery*. December 19, 1999.

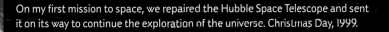
On my first mission to space, we repaired the Hubble Space Telescope and sent it on its way to continue the exploration of the universe. Christmas Day, 1999.

Left to right: me, Dima Kondratyev, and Sasha Kaleri awaiting water survival training on the deck of a Russian naval vessel in the Black Sea. September 11, 2001. I learned of the terrorist attacks in New York and Washington, D.C., when the ship returned to port.

Putting on my harness before entering space shuttle *Endeavour* as the commander of STS-118. August 8, 2007.

My STS-118 crew and the crew of the space station in the U.S. laboratory module. From left to right and front to back: Clay Anderson, Fyodor Yurchikhin (Russia), Oleg Kotov (Russia), Al Drew, Barbara Morgan, Dave Williams (Canada), me, Charlie Hobaugh, Rick Mastracchio, and Tracy Caldwell. August 2007.

My daughters, Samantha (top) and Charlotte, in Red Square, Moscow. Summer 2008.

My fiancée, Amiko Kauderer, and me in Red Square. March 2015.

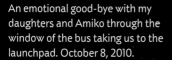

An emotional good-bye with my daughters and Amiko through the window of the bus taking us to the launchpad. October 8, 2010.

Hanging out of our crew quarters in Node 2 of the ISS. From left: Doug Wheelock, me on the "ceiling," Shannon Walker, and Oleg Skripochka on the "floor." November 2010.

Getting in the Christmas spirit for my second holiday in space. December 2010.

Our charred Soyuz capsule on its side in the Kazakhstan snow after our crew had been removed. March 16, 2011.

From left: Oleg, Sasha, and I are bundled up after our landing in the middle of a Kazakhstan blizzard. March 16, 2011.

Thinking about my coming yearlong space mission from inside a Soyuz simulator at the Gagarin Cosmonaut Training Center outside of Moscow. February 2015.

Our Soyuz spacecraft lifts off toward space and the ISS. March 28, 2015.

My feet get in the way as I admire the unmistakable blue waters of the Bahamas from the Cupola aboard the ISS. Fall 2015.

On the ISS with my crewmates Anton Shkaplerov (left), Samantha Cristoforetti (center), and Terry Virts celebrating Samantha's birthday. April 26, 2015.

My phony juggling act with an assist from zero gravity: the fruit had been sent to the ISS on the Japanese HTV resupply vehicle. August 2015.

Kjell Lindgen in the U.S. laboratory module demonstrating the joys of living in zero gravity. August 2015.

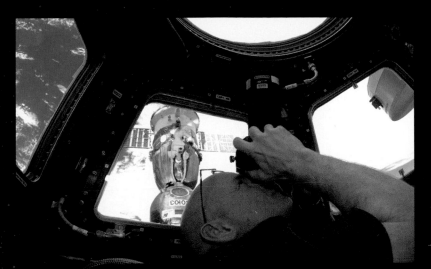

Me taking a photo of the Earth from the Cupola, with the docked Soyuz visible through the window.

One of my favorite places to admire off Earth, our Milky Way galaxy.

Me (barely visible), Gennady Padalka, and Misha Kornienko inside the very crowded Soyuz capsule. March 2, 2016.

Our Soyuz spacecraft as it crashes back onto Earth. March 2, 2016.

Brothers and best friends—then and now. Above: Mark and me in New Jersey, circa 1968. Below: separated by glass to protect me from germs before my Year in Space launch. March 2015.

My formal NASA photograph taken in the EMU (Extravehicular Activity Mobility Unit, or spacewalking spacesuit) just prior to my Year in Space mission. Late 2014.

ing together are so loud we have trouble hearing one another. I had remembered this about my previous mission to the ISS, of course, but still I can't believe it's so noisy. I can't believe I'll ever get used to it.

"I realized a few minutes ago, Misha," I say, "that our lives without noise have ceased to exist."

"Guys," Gennady says. *"Tselyi god!"* An entire year!

"Ne napominai, Gena," answers Misha. Gena, don't remind me.

Now we are in the rendezvous stage. Joining two objects in two different orbits traveling at different speeds (in this case, the Soyuz and the ISS) is a long process. It's one we understand well and have been through many times, but still it's a delicate maneuver.

After MECO, we can unstrap ourselves, but there isn't really anywhere to go.

In a few hours we will be docking. Gennady opens his manual to the appropriate pages and starts punching buttons. The process is largely automated, but he needs to stay on top of it in case something goes wrong and he has to take over.

When it's time for the docking probe to deploy, nothing happens. We wait. Gennady says something to Russian mission control in rapid-fire Russian. They respond, sounding annoyed, then garble into static. We are not sure if they heard us. We are still a long way from ISS.

This could be a problem.

The three of us give one another a look, an international I-can't-believe-this look. Soon, ISS will be looming in the window, its eight solar array wings glinting in the sun like the legs of a giant insect. But without the docking probe, we won't be able to connect to it and climb aboard. We'll have to return to Earth.

Depending on when the next Soyuz will be ready, we might have to wait weeks or months. We could miss our chance altogether.

We think about the prospect of coming back to Earth, how ridiculous we'll feel climbing out of this capsule, saying hello again to people we've just said the biggest good-bye in the world to. Comm with the ground is intermittent, so they can't help us much in our efforts to figure out what's going on. I turn to see Misha's face. He is shaking his head in disappointment.

Once Gennady and Misha transition to a different software program, we see that the probe is in fact deployed. It was just a software "funny."

All three of us sigh with relief. This day hasn't been for nothing. We are still going to the space station.

When we finally make contact with the station, we hear and feel the eerie sound of the probe hitting, then scratching its way into the opening, a grinding metal-on-metal sound that ends with a satisfying clunk. Now hooks are driven through the docking port to reinforce the connection. We've made it. We slap one another on the arms.

We struggle out of the Sokol suits we put on nearly ten hours earlier and put our wet diapers in a Russian wet trash bag for later disposal on the ISS. We are tired and sweaty but excited to be attached to our new home. I get into the blue flight suit I call my Captain America suit because of the huge American flag emblazoned across the front.

As eager as we are to greet our new crewmates, we need to make sure the seal between the Soyuz and ISS is good. The leak checks take nearly two hours. If we don't have a good seal, opening the hatch will cause ISS and Soyuz to lose their air. Occasionally, as we wait, we hear the crew on the other side banging on the hatch in a friendly greeting. We bang back.

The leak check finally complete, Gennady opens the hatch on our side. Anton Shkaplerov, the only cosmonaut on board the ISS, opens the Russian hatch on their side. I smell something strangely familiar and unmistakable, a strong burned metal smell, like the smell of sparklers on the Fourth of July. Objects that have been exposed to the vacuum of space have this unique smell on them, like the smell of welding—the smell of space.

Besides Anton, there are two people up here already: the commander and the only other American, Terry Virts, and an Italian astronaut representing the European Space Agency, Samantha Cristoforetti. I know them all, some much better than others. Soon, we will all know one another much better.

Over the course of this year in space, Misha and I will see a total of thirteen other people come and go. We hope that the change in crew members will help break up the mission and the monotony to make our year less challenging.

Unlike the early days of spaceflight, when piloting skill was what mattered, twenty-first-century astronauts are chosen for our ability to perform a lot of different jobs and to get along well with others, especially in stressful and cramped circumstances for long periods of time. Each of my crewmates is not only a close co-worker, but also a roommate and a surrogate for all humanity.

Gennady floats through the hatch first and hugs Anton. These greetings are always jubilant—we know exactly who we're going to see when we open the hatch, but still it's somehow startling to launch off the Earth, travel to space, and find friends already living up here. As Gennady and Anton say their hellos, Misha and I are waiting our turns. We know that many people on the ground are watching, including our families. There is a live feed playing for everyone at Baikonur, as well as in mission control in Houston and online. Suddenly I get an idea and turn to Misha.

"Let's go through together," I suggest. "As a show of solidarity."

"Good idea, my brother. We are in this together."

It's a bit awkward floating through the small hatch together, but the gesture gets a big smile from everyone on the other side.

Misha and I float through the hatch together as we enter the ISS for day one of our year in space. March 28, 2015.

Our families in Baikonur are waiting to have a conference call with us, which we'll do from the Russian service module. I float down there and make a wrong turn. It's weird to be back here— floating through the station is so familiar, but it's also disorienting. It's only day one.

As the smell of space dissipates, I'm starting to detect the unique aroma of the ISS, as familiar as the smell of my childhood home. It is mostly the off-gassing from the equipment and everything else, which on Earth we call the new-car smell. Up here the scent is stronger because the plastic particles are weightless, as is the air, so they mingle in every breath. There is also the faint scent of garbage and a whiff of body odor. Even though we seal up the trash as well as we can, we get rid of it only every few months, when an emptied resupply craft becomes a garbage truck.

The sound of fans and the hum of electronics are both loud and inescapable. I feel like I have to raise my voice to be heard above the noise, though I know from experience I'll get used to it. This part of the Russian segment is especially loud. It's dark and a bit cold as well. I feel a shiver of realization: I'm going to be up here for nearly a year. What exactly have I gotten myself into? It occurs to me for a moment that this might be one of the stupider things I've ever done.

Once we get situated in the Russian side of the space station, we have a video conference with our families. During the call, they can see and hear us, but we can only hear them. There is a loud echo. The comm configuration up here is slightly off. I hear Charlotte telling me what the launch was like; then I talk briefly to Samantha and then to Amiko. It's great to hear their voices. But I'm conscious that my Russian colleagues are waiting to talk to their families, too.

Once we finish the call, I head down to the U.S. segment with Terry and Samantha, where I'm going to spend the better part of the year to come. Though ISS is all one facility, for the most part the Russians live and work on their side and everyone else lives and works on the other side—"the U.S. segment."

Terry and Samantha show me around, reminding me how things work up here now. They start with the most important piece of equipment to master: the toilet, also known as the Waste and Hygiene Compartment, or WHC. We also run through a quick safety brief that we will redo more thoroughly in a couple of days once I'm more settled. An emergency could strike at any time—fire, ammonia leak, depressurization—and I'll have to be ready to deal with whatever comes, even on day one.

We head back to the Russian segment for a traditional welcoming party—special dinners are held there every Friday night and on other special occasions, including holidays, birthdays, and good-bye dinners before each Soyuz leaves. Welcoming parties are one of those occasions, and Terry has warmed up my favorite, barbecued beef, which I stick to a tortilla using the surface tension of the barbecue sauce (we eat tortillas because of their long shelf life and lack of crumbs). We also have the traditional foods we share at Friday-night dinners—lump crabmeat and black caviar. Everyone is in a festive mood. Eventually we say our good-nights, and Terry, Samantha, and I head back to the U.S. segment.

I find my crew quarters, or CQ, the one part on the space station that will belong just to me. It's about the size of an old-fashioned phone booth. My crew quarters on board the ISS will be my home away from home for my year in space.

Four CQs are arranged in Node 2: floor, ceiling, left wall, and right wall. I'm on the left wall this time; last time I was on the ceiling. The CQ is clean and empty, and I know that over the course of the next year it will fill with clutter, like any other home. I zip myself into my sleeping bag, making a special point to appreciate that it's brand-new. Though I will replace the liner a couple of times, the bag itself won't be cleaned or replaced for a whole year. I turn off the light and close my eyes. Sleeping while floating isn't easy, especially when you're out of practice. Even though my eyes are closed, cosmic flashes occasionally light up my field of vision, the result of radiation striking my retinas, creating the illusion of light. This phenomenon was first noticed by astronauts during the Apollo era, and its cause still isn't thoroughly understood. I'll get used to this, too, but for now the flashes are an alarming reminder of the radiation zipping through my brain. As I drift off into a restless haze, it occurs to me that this is the first of 340 times I will have to fall asleep here.

Training myself to sleep while floating upright was hard.

14

MY GOAL FOR most of my adult life has been to pilot aircraft and spacecraft. So it sometimes strikes me as odd that the International Space Station doesn't need to be piloted at all. We don't fly the space station—it's controlled by computers, and even if human intervention is needed, it can be controlled by laptops on board or the ground. We live in the space station, the way you live in a building. We work in it, the way scientists work in a laboratory. And we also work *on* it, the way mechanics work on a boat, if the boat were adrift in international waters and the Coast Guard had no way to reach it.

I sometimes see the station described as an object: "The International Space Station is the most expensive object ever created." But when you live inside the station for months, it doesn't feel like an object. It feels like a *place,* a very specific place with an inside and an outside and rooms upon rooms. Each room has its own purpose, its own equipment and hardware, and its own feeling and smell distinct from the others. Each module has its own story and its own quirks.

I've been on station for a week now. I'm getting better at knowing where I am when I first wake up. If I have a headache, I know it's because I've drifted too far from the vent blowing clean air at my face. I'm often still disoriented about my body position. I'll wake up convinced that I'm upside down, because in the dark and without gravity, my inner ear just takes a random guess as to how my body is positioned in the small space. When I turn on a light, it seems like the room is rotating rapidly as it reorients itself around me, though I know it's actually my brain readjusting to what I am seeing.

The light in my crew quarters takes a minute to warm up to full brightness. The space is just barely big enough for me and my sleeping bag, two laptops, some clothes, toiletries, photos of Amiko and my daughters, and a few paperback books.

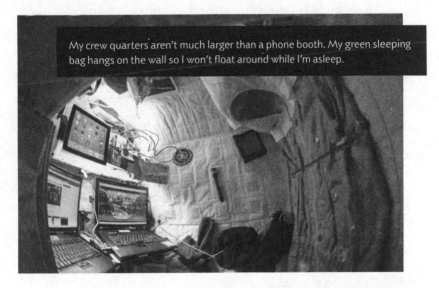

My crew quarters aren't much larger than a phone booth. My green sleeping bag hangs on the wall so I won't float around while I'm asleep.

Without getting out of my sleeping bag, I wake up one of the two computers attached to the wall by tapping on the space-bar. Then I look at my schedule for today. I click through new emails, stretch and yawn, then fish around in my toiletries bag, attached to the wall down by my left knee, for my toothpaste and toothbrush. I brush, still in my sleeping bag, then swallow the toothpaste and chase it with a sip of water out of a bag with a straw. There isn't really a good way to spit in space.

I spend a few minutes looking over the daily summary sent up by the Mission Control Center in Houston. This is an electronic document that shows the state of the space station and its systems, asks us questions they came up with overnight, and includes important notes for the work planned for that day. There's also a cartoon at the end, often making fun of either us or themselves. Today's daily summary shows many challenges to tackle. These are the days I look forward to.

Mission control schedules our days into different time slots, which can be as short as five minutes, using a program called OSTPV (Onboard Short Term Plan Viewer). This program, like a digital daily planner, rules our lives. Throughout the day, a dotted red line moves relentlessly across the OSTPV window on my laptop, pushing through the block of time mission control has estimated for each task. If I take longer than scheduled to complete a task, like repairing equipment, the extra time has to come out of something else on the schedule—a meal, my exercise time, the brief time I get to myself at the end of the day (which OSTPV labels "pre-sleep"), or—worst of all—sleep. For Terry, Samantha, and me, much of today is to be taken up with one long task labeled DRAGON CAPTURE.

From the outside, the International Space Station looks like a number of giant empty soda cans attached to one another end to end. The length of the station is made up of five modules connected the long way—three American and two Russian. More modules, including ones from Europe and Japan as well as the

United States, are connected on either side, and the Russians have three that are attached up and down. (We call these directions zenith and nadir.) Between my first mission to the space station and this one, it has grown by seven modules, all planned out from the very beginning of the project in the 1990s. Whenever resupply vehicles are berthed here, for a time there is a new "room." Those rooms get roomier as we get the cargo unpacked, then get smaller again as we fill them with trash. After we detach them from the station, they burn up in the atmosphere—except for the relatively new SpaceX Dragon, which can return to Earth intact and be reused.

Tim Kopra and I "take out the trash" when we release the Cygnus full of our garbage to burn up in the atmosphere. February 2016.

The fact that we can't step outside when we feel like it is one of the things that some people find hard to imagine about living on the space station. Putting on a spacesuit and leaving the station for a spacewalk is an hours-long process that requires the full attention of at least three people on station and dozens more on the ground. Spacewalks are the most dangerous thing we do on orbit.

Even if the station is on fire, even if it's filling up with poisonous gas, even if a meteoroid has crashed through a module and our air is rushing out, the only way to escape the station is in a Soyuz capsule, which also needs preparation and planning to depart safely. We practice dealing with emergency scenarios regularly, and in many of these drills, we race to prepare the Soyuz as quickly as we can. No one has ever had to use the Soyuz as a lifeboat, and we hope this never happens. But we need to be as ready as possible, just in case.

The space station is an international effort and a shared facility, but I spend almost all of my time on the cluster of modules—together with American and Japanese visiting vehicles—we call the U.S. operational segment. My cosmonaut colleagues spend the majority of their time on the Russian segment, made up of the Russian modules as well as the visiting Russian Progress and Soyuz spacecraft.

The module where I spend a lot of my day is formally named Destiny, but we mostly just call it "the lab." It's a state-of-the-art scientific laboratory with walls, floors, and ceiling packed with equipment. Because there is no gravity, every surface is usable storage space. The lab looks cluttered—people with OCD would probably have trouble living and working here. But the things I use most I can put my hands on in seconds.

There are also many things I would *not* be able to put my hands on if asked—without gravity, items wander off regularly. The ground will often email us WANTED posters for lost objects, like the ones the FBI puts in post offices. Occasionally one of us will find a tool or part that has been missing for years. Eight years is the record, so far, for a missing object reappearing.

Most of the spaces where I spend my time have no windows and no natural light, just very bright fluorescent lights and clinical white walls. Without any earthly light, the modules seem cold and spare, like a prison of sorts. Because the sun rises and sets every ninety minutes as we circle the planet, we can't use it to keep track of time. So without my watch keeping me on Greenwich Mean Time and a schedule tightly structuring my days, I'd be completely lost.

It's hard to explain to people who haven't lived here how much we start to miss nature. In the future, there will be a word for the specific kind of nostalgia we feel for living things. We all like to listen to recordings of nature—rain forests, birdcalls, wind in the trees. As sterile and lifeless as everything is up here, we do have windows that give us a fantastic view of Earth. It's hard to describe the experience of looking down at the planet. I feel as though I know the Earth in an intimate way most people don't— the coastline, terrain, mountains, and rivers. Some parts of the world, especially in Asia, are so blanketed by air pollution that they appear sick, in need of treatment or at least a chance to heal. The line of our atmosphere on the horizon looks as thin as a contact lens over an eye, and its fragility seems to demand our protection.

One of my favorite views of the Earth is of the Bahamas—a large island chain with a stunning contrast from light to dark colors. The vibrant deep blue of the ocean mixes with a much brighter turquoise swirled with something almost like gold, where the sun bounces off the sandy shallows and reefs. Whenever new crewmates come up to the station for the first time, I make a point of taking them to the Cupola to see the Bahamas. That sight always reminds me to stop and appreciate the view of the Earth I've been given the privilege of seeing.

Me looking out a window in the Cupola, my favorite place on the ISS.

Since before the space shuttle was retired, NASA has been working with private companies to develop spacecraft to supply the station with cargo. At some point in the future, they may even bring up new crews. The most successful private company so far has been SpaceX, which produces the Dragon spacecraft. Yesterday, a Dragon launched successfully from Cape Canaveral. Since then, it has been in orbit a safe ten kilometers (6.2 miles) from us. This morning, April 17, our aim is to capture it with the space station's robot arm and attach it to the berthing port on station. The process of grappling a visiting vehicle is a bit like playing an arcade claw machine, except that it involves real equipment worth millions of dollars flying at impossible speeds. Not only could an error cause us to lose or damage Dragon and the valuable supplies on board, but a slip of the hand could crash the visiting vehicle into the station. A Progress cargo spacecraft once struck the old Russian space station *Mir*, and its crew was lucky not to have been killed by the rapid loss of atmosphere.

These uncrewed rockets are the only means by which we can get adequate supplies from Earth. Right now, Dragon is carrying 4,300 pounds of food, water, and oxygen; spare parts and supplies for the systems that keep us alive; health-care supplies; clothing; and towels and washcloths, all of which we throw away after using them for as long as we can. Dragon will also be bringing new science experiments for us to carry out, as well as new samples to keep the existing ones going. In addition, each uncrewed rocket carries small care packages from our families, which we always look forward to, and precious fresh food that we enjoy for just a few days, until it runs out or goes bad. Fruits and vegetables seem to rot faster here than on Earth. I'm not sure why, and seeing the process makes me worry that the same thing is happening to my own cells.

We are especially looking forward to this Dragon's arrival because another uncrewed rocket, built by a different company, exploded just after launch back in October. The station is always stocked far beyond the needs of the current crew, so there was no immediate danger of running out of food or oxygen when those supplies were lost. Still, this was the first time a rocket to resupply ISS had failed in years, and it destroyed millions of dollars' worth of equipment. And the loss of vital supplies like food and oxygen made everyone think harder about what would happen if a string of failures were to occur.

I get dressed while I skim over the procedures for the Dragon capture again. We all trained for this thoroughly before launch, capturing many imaginary Dragons using a simulator, so I'm just refreshing my recollection. Getting dressed is a bit of a hassle when you can't sit or stand, but I've gotten used to it. The most challenging thing is putting on my socks without gravity to help me bend over. It's not a challenge to figure out what to wear, since I wear the same thing every day: a pair of khaki pants with lots of pockets and strips of Velcro across the thighs, crucial when you can't put anything down. I have decided to experiment with how long I can make my clothes last, the idea of going to Mars in the back of my mind. Can a pair of underwear be worn four days instead of two? Can a pair of socks last a month? Can a pair of pants last six months? I aim to find out. I put on my favorite black T-shirt and a sweatshirt that, because it's flying with me for the third time, has to be one of the most traveled pieces of clothing in the history of clothing.

Dressed and ready for breakfast, I open the door to my CQ. As I push against the back wall to float myself out, I accidentally kick loose a paperback book: *Endurance: Shackleton's Incredible Voyage,* by Alfred Lansing. I brought this book with me on my previous flight as well, and sometimes I flip through it after a long day and reflect on what these Antarctic explorers went through almost exactly a hundred years before. Their ship became trapped by the ice and sunk, leaving the twenty-eight-man crew stranded on ice floes for months, forced to kill their dogs for food, and nearly frozen to death in the biting cold. They survived the longest open boat journey across stormy violent seas and hiked across mountains that had been considered impassable to reach a remote whaling station and rescue. Remarkably, after an almost two-year ordeal, not a single member of the expedition was lost.

When I try to put myself in their place, the doubt about their survival must have been worse than the hunger and the cold. When I read about their experiences, I think about how much harder they had it than I do. If I start to feel sorry for myself because I miss my family or because I had a frustrating day or because the isolation is getting to me, reading a few pages about the Shackleton expedition reminds me that even if I have it hard up here in some ways, I'm certainly not going through what they did.

Out in Node 1, the module that serves largely as our kitchen and living room, I open a food container attached to the wall and fish out a pouch of dehydrated coffee with cream and sugar. I float over to the hot water dispenser in the ceiling of the lab, which works by inserting a needle into a nozzle on the bag. When the bag is full, I replace the needle with a drinking straw equipped with a valve to pinch it closed. It was oddly unsatisfying at first to drink coffee from a plastic bag sipped through a straw, but now I'm not bothered by it. I flip through the breakfast options and choose some dehydrated eggs, which are made by adding hot water. Then I warm up some irradiated sausage links in the food warmer box, which resembles a metal briefcase. I cut the bag open, then clean the scissors by licking them, since we have no sink (we each have our own scissors). I spoon the eggs out of the bag onto a tortilla—conveniently, surface tension holds them in place—add the sausage and some hot sauce, roll it up, and eat the breakfast burrito while catching up with the morning's news on CNN. All the while I'm holding myself in place with my right big toe tucked ever so slightly under a handrail on the floor. Handrails are placed on the walls, floors, and ceilings of every module and at the hatches where modules connect, allowing us to propel ourselves through the modules or to stay in place rather than drifting away.

Terry Virts and I enjoying lunch in Node 1, our living room and dining room in one. April 2015.

There are a lot of things about living in weightlessness that are fun, but eating is not one of them. I miss being able to sit in a chair while eating a meal, relaxing and pausing to connect with other people. Eating on the space station, at my workplace, three times a day, while constantly floating and steadying myself, is hardly the same. The table we use for eating has Velcro strips and duct tape to help us keep things in place, but it's still a challenge to manage all these items that may float away. I bite an escaped coffee sphere out of the air and swallow it before it can drift into a piece of equipment, or onto a crewmate or my pants (as they need to last six months).

As I'm eating, Terry floats in and wishes me a good morning while looking for coffee. He loves baseball, so there's always a game on some laptop, especially when the Astros or the Orioles are playing. I've gotten used to the rhythm of the nine-inning games marking time for a few hours of our workday.

Terry eats a maple muffin top while I'm finishing my egg burrito. Next my crewmates and I meet in the U.S. lab for the daily planning conference (DPC) with mission control in Houston, people at other NASA sites, and their counterparts in Russia, Japan, and Europe. The conference generally starts at 7:30 a.m. our time. Once we are all assembled in the Russian segment, Terry grabs the microphone from its position Velcroed to the wall.

"Houston, station on Space to Ground One, we are ready for the DPC."

Mission control answers with a bright "Good morning, station!" even though it's 2:30 a.m. in Houston. We go over the day's plans for a few minutes, mostly about Dragon capture. When we are done with Houston, they hand us over to the Marshall Space

Flight Center, in Huntsville, Alabama. Then Huntsville hands us over to Munich so we can coordinate with the European Space Agency. Then we talk to "J-COM" in the Japanese mission control in Tsukuba, Japan. Then it's time to talk to Russia: Terry turns it over to the cosmonauts by saying *"Dobroye utro, Tsup va Moskvy, Anton pozhaluysta."* ("Good morning, Control Center Moscow. Anton, please.") Then Anton takes over the mic because he's in charge in the Russian segment, and he leads the planning meeting with the Russians.

All of this coordinating with sites all over the world might sound time-consuming, and it can be, but no one would ever suggest changing it. With so many space agencies cooperating, it's important that everyone knows what everyone else is doing. Plans can change quickly, and a misunderstanding could be costly, or deadly. We do this whole circuit of control centers both morning and evening, five days a week. I've chosen not to think about how many times I'll do these before I come back to Earth.

Dragon is in its orbit ten kilometers (6.2 miles) away from us, matching our speed of 17,500 miles per hour. We can see its light blinking at us on the external cameras. Soon, SpaceX mission control in Hawthorne, California, will move it to within two kilometers (1.2 miles). Then authority transfers to mission control in Houston, and NASA authorizes it to move to within 350 meters, then 250 meters, then 30 meters, and finally the capture point at 10 meters. Once Dragon is close enough, Samantha will capture it with one of the station's robot arms. This is a glacially slow and deliberate process—one of the many things that's very different between movies and real life. In the films *Interstellar* and *2001: A Space Odyssey,* a visiting spacecraft zips up to a space station and locks on to it, a hatch pops open, and people pass through, all over the course of about a few minutes. In reality, we operate with the knowledge that one spacecraft is always a potentially fatal threat to another—a bigger threat the closer it gets—and so we move with extreme caution.

Samantha is going to operate the robot arm from the robotics workstation in the Cupola today. Terry will be her backup, and I will be helping out with the approach and rendezvous procedures. Terry and I squeeze in with her, watching the data screen that shows the speed and position of Dragon.

Samantha Cristoforetti is one of the few women to have served as a fighter pilot in the Italian Air Force. She is also friendly and quick to laugh, and she has a rare talent for languages. She's fluent in English and Russian, the two official languages of the ISS—she sometimes acts as an interpreter between cosmonauts and astronauts if we have to talk about something nuanced or complicated. She also speaks French, German, and her native Italian, and she's working on learning Chinese.

Before Samantha left Earth, she took Terry to her hair salon in Houston so her stylist could teach him how to cut her sleek hairstyle in space. Haircuts are one of the many tasks ISS crew members have to do for one another, so Terry, the upcoming commander of the ISS, was being trained as a temporary hairstylist. Their lesson was a big hit on social media. Halfway through their mission together, the big day came. Because we can't leave bits of hair floating in the air for others to inhale, our haircut equipment includes a vacuum cleaner. Terry tried his very best, but he still screwed it up—the layers that Samantha's stylist had made seem so easy to replicate under Earth's gravity were now floating all over the place. Samantha has spent the rest of her mission with her thick, dark hair sticking out from her head in a way that reminds me of a gorilla's fur.

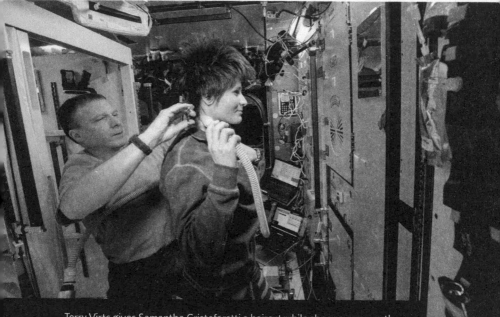

Terry Virts gives Samantha Cristoforetti a haircut while she vacuums up the loose hairs. March 2015.

The capcom speaking to us on the ground today is David Saint-Jacques, a Canadian astronaut. The term "capcom" is left over from the early days of the Mercury program when the astronauts went to space in capsules and one person in mission control was designated the "capsule communicator," the only person to talk with the astronaut in space. "Capsule communicator" was shortened to "capcom," and the name stuck. Today David is talking us through the capture process, announcing Dragon's position as it moves, controlled by the ground.

"Station, Houston, on Space to Ground Two. Dragon is inside the two-hundred-meter keep-out sphere." The keep-out sphere is an imaginary safety zone around the station, meant to protect us from accidental collisions. "The crew now has the authority to issue an abort." This means that we can stop the process ourselves if we lose contact with Houston or if Dragon is outside the approach corridor.

"Houston on Two for rendezvous," Terry says. "Houston, capture conditions are confirmed. We're ready for Dragon capture."

"Copy that, stand by for capture."

When the Dragon is within ten meters (twenty feet), Samantha takes control of the robotic arm.

"Station on Two for rendezvous," we hear from mission control. "You are go for capture sequence."

"Station copies," Samantha answers.

Samantha reaches out with the robot arm, watching a monitor that shows Dragon's position and speed. She can also look out the big Cupola windows to see what she's doing. She moves the robot arm out away from the station—very slowly and deliberately. On the center screen, Dragon grows larger and larger. The arm creeps out slowly, slowly. It's almost touching Dragon.

Samantha pulls the trigger. "Capture," she says.

Perfect.

"Capture confirmed at five-fifty-five a.m. Central Time, while the station and Dragon fly over the northern Pacific Ocean, just to the east of Japan."

Samantha's round face has been a study of concentration.

The moment capture is confirmed, her face relaxes into a huge smile and she high-fives Terry and me.

Terry speaks: "Houston, capture is complete. Samantha did a perfect job grappling Dragon."

"Copy and concur. Great job, guys. Congratulations."

The danger Dragon poses to the station is not over. The process of pressurizing the space between Dragon and the station (the "vestibule") takes several hours and is important to do correctly. A mistake in this procedure could cause depressurization.

After a number of steps, we declare the seal safe, but we will wait until tomorrow to open the hatch. I've seen crews push themselves to get through the entire process because they were eager to get into their care packages and fresh food. But opening the hatch takes hours, and after the morning we spent with capture, there's too much risk of making a mistake. Once the hatch is open, it will take the whole crew five weeks to unload all the cargo.

15

When I float into my CQ for a moment to check my email, it's the first time I've had the chance to pause and think today. I can tell the CO_2 level is high right now. My struggle with carbon dioxide has been going on as long as I've been flying in space. It wasn't until I was a month or so into my first mission aboard the space station that I started to connect the symptoms I was feeling to high levels of CO_2. At two millimeters of pressure I feel okay, but at around three, I get headaches and start to feel congested. At four, my eyes burn and I can feel the fuzzy brain effect. If I'm trying to do something complex, I actually start to feel stupid, which is a dangerous way to feel on a space station. We never know when an emergency situation may arise, so we have to be sharp at all times.

Navy submarines turn on their air scrubbers when the CO_2 concentration rises above two millimeters of pressure, even though the scrubbers are noisy and risk giving away the submarine's secret location. That's how important they think low CO_2 levels are. By comparison, the international agreement on ISS says we have no problem up to six millimeters of pressure! I feel that NASA should have the same standards as the Navy.

The ISS uses a device called the Carbon Dioxide Removal Assembly (CDRA, pronounced "Seedra") to control CO_2. It has become my biggest nemesis. There are two of them—each weighs about five hundred pounds and looks something like a car engine.

When it is functioning properly, the Seedra is a marvel of engineering—either dumping the extra CO_2 into space or working with another device called Sabatier to create fresh drinking water. But the Seedra is a finicky beast that requires a lot of care and feeding to keep it operating. Working on a complex piece of hardware in space is infinitely harder than it would be on Earth, where I

Terry Virts and I fix the Seedra, my nemesis, during my year in space. July 2015.

could put down tools and parts and they'd stay put. And there are so many complex pieces of hardware up here—NASA estimates that we spend a quarter of our time on maintenance and repairs.

On this mission, the two Seedras have had a lot of issues. If we are going to get to Mars, we are going to need a much better way to deal with CO_2. Using our current unreliable system, a Mars crew would be in significant danger.

The last daily planning conference of the day is held at 7:30 p.m., and dinnertime is shortly after that. As it's a Friday, we are looking forward to sharing a group dinner in the Russian segment, as always.

I gather my things to bring to Friday dinner in a big ziplock bag. I pack my own spoon and my own scissors for opening food bags. I pack foods to share, stuff from the bonus food container I brought up with me: canned trout, some irradiated Mexican meat, and a processed cheese similar to Cheez Whiz that Gennady loves. The Russians always share some tarry black caviar, for which I've developed a real taste, as well as some canned lobster meat. Samantha always brings good snacks, too—the Europeans have the best food.

With my goodie bag under my arm, I float down the FGB, then into the service module. There I find Gennady and Samantha watching a movie on a laptop while Anton floats horizontally to them, finishing up an experiment on the wall. In English, Gennady welcomes me and thanks me for the food I've brought. Misha emerges from the bathroom. Terry shows up with his own goodie bag and greets us.

Anton and Misha acted as though Gennady were in charge as soon as he was on board, even though Anton is officially the Russian segment lead. Things simply seem to go better when Gennady is around, and everyone looks up to him as a natural leader.

Misha has been great to fly with so far, too. What's most important to him is friendship and camaraderie, and he brings a positive energy to everything he does.

I'm often asked how well we get along with the Russians, and people never quite seem to believe me when I say there are no issues. It's true we don't always understand each other. To Americans, Russians can at first seem stony and unfriendly, while to Russians, Americans at first come across as naïve and weak. But we who have chosen to live on this space station together have to trust one another with our lives and must put aside cultural conflicts. We have agreed to carry out this huge and challenging project together, so we work to understand and see the best in one another.

It's challenging for six people to eat together in such a small space, but we look forward to this chance to have a meal as a crew. We talk about how our work has gone during the week. We talk about our families and catch up on current events in our respective countries. If there is significant news involving both the United States and Russia, for instance our two countries' involvement in Syria, we'll touch on it lightly, but no one wants to go into any detail.

Our dining room table hangs off the wall at an angle to save space. There are different kinds of food packages, silver bags with beverages, and yellow bags labeled with our names that hold our personal utensils.

Friday-night dinners always include dessert. Russian space dessert is almost always just a can of stewed apples. We have much more variety on the U.S. segment, though our desserts aren't gourmet level. The cherry blueberry cobbler is one of my favorites, and the chocolate pudding is always a big hit with the Russians, so I've brought some to share. It drives me nuts that our food specialists insist on giving us the same number of chocolate, vanilla, and butterscotch puddings, when the laws of physics dictate chocolate will disappear much faster. No one gets a vanilla craving in space (or on Earth).

We say our good-nights and float back to the U.S. segment, remembering to bring our spoons, scissors, and leftovers with us. Back in my CQ, I look through the plan for tomorrow, Saturday. As often happens up here, work will continue into the weekend, and I will do my required exercise sessions as well. I take off my pants and secure them under a bungee cord, don't bother changing my shirt, and brush my teeth. I put on my headset and call Amiko to talk for a few minutes before going to sleep. It's still early in the evening for her. I tell her about Dragon capture, and she tells me about her workday. She has also been helping my daughter Samantha and running errands for my father. I'm lucky to have Amiko taking care of things for me on the ground, and sometimes it bugs me that I can never do much to help her. This year in space is a test of endurance for Amiko as well, and it's important for me to remember that.

It's strange waking up here on weekends, even more so than waking up other days, because on weekends it becomes clearer that

I'm sleeping at my workplace. I wake up Saturday and I'm still at work; wake up on Sunday, still at work. Months later, I'll still be here. On the weekends, we are usually given time to do personal things—videoconference with family, catch up with personal email, read, and get the rest we need to start another week of long days of challenging work.

But there is a certain amount of mission creep into our time on weekends. A couple of hours of exercise on at least one day of the weekend are mandatory, since the damage to our bodies caused by weightlessness does not take a break for weekends or holidays. And there is station maintenance that can't be left until Monday, or that we won't have time to do when Monday comes around. The weekend is also when we clean, and cleaning is a bit more involved in zero gravity. On Earth, dust and lint and hair and fingernail clippings and bits of food *fall,* so dusting and vacuuming get rid of pretty much everything. On the space station, a piece of dirt can wind up on the wall, the ceiling, or attached to an expensive piece of equipment. A lot of crap gets caught in the filters of the ventilation system, and when too much of it builds up, our air quality is affected. Because the walls get dirty and wet, mold is a concern. And because mold spores don't fall to the floor but linger in our breathable air, they can pose a serious health risk. As a result, we are expected to clean most everything on station we regularly touch every weekend, with a vacuum and antiseptic wipes. We also take samples from the walls to grow in petri dishes and send back to Earth for analysis. So far, they haven't found anything toxic, but it's both disgusting and fascinating to see what's living on the walls.

This Saturday, we also need to start unpacking Dragon's

cargo. Once everyone is up and ready, Terry and Samantha meet me in Node 2. We put on goggles and dust masks before opening Dragon's hatch to protect us from dust and debris that might be floating inside. Then we arm ourselves with checklists and cameras to document each step of our work for later analysis by NASA and SpaceX, and a video camera so mission control can see exactly what we're doing in real time. When we're ready, we call down to the ground so they can follow along with us.

When Samantha opens the ISS hatch that leads to Dragon and slides it out of the way, we are greeted by the slightly burnt smell of space. We start unloading and everything goes just as planned. We now have 4,300 pounds of cargo to unload. Our care packages are clearly marked and easily accessible once we open the hatch, as are the fresh food, and ice cream. Terry and I hand out the packages to everyone, feeling a bit like Santa Claus.

The fresh food bags contain apples, pears, red peppers, and green peppers. They smell great. We will eat them at every meal for the next few days before they spoil.

All the cargo we unload from Dragon must be packed into fabric bags and labeled with bar codes, just like food in a grocery store, as well as a printed list of what's in each and where it goes within the ISS. It's so easy to lose stuff up here that if we were to put something in the wrong place, we may never see it again. This makes the work of unpacking Dragon both tedious and stressful. After spending a few hours unloading Dragon, I notice that my arms smell like space.

Since it's Saturday, I have a bit more time to make personal phone calls to friends and family. I've found myself thinking about my mother today—it's been three years since she died, and I'm wishing she could see what I'm doing up here. She was so proud of Mark and me when we became astronauts, and she came to all six of our launches at Cape Canaveral. Seeing her set herself an incredibly tough goal—to pass the men's physical fitness test to join the police department—and then to conquer it was worth more than all the pep talks in the world. Her accomplishment wasn't meant to be instructional for Mark and me, but it was.

When I get a chance to float into my CQ, I see that Amiko has emailed me. She put some flowers on my mother's grave today and took a picture to include in the email. I'm moved by Amiko's gesture. She has a lot to deal with on the weekends, but she remembered this date and drove out to the cemetery to do this because I couldn't.

We continue to unpack Dragon on Sunday. I work through a few bags of medical supplies, clothes, and food. I'm taking a break to do some cleaning—it's still Sunday, after all—and not long afterward I hear a fire alarm.

Astronauts do not scare easily, and this alarm does not exactly scare me, but it certainly gets my attention. Fire is on the short list of things that can kill you in space incredibly quickly. A fire on the old Russian space station *Mir* blinded and choked the crew within seconds, and if it hadn't been for their quick reaction, they could have died. Some of the older cosmonauts, including Gennady, refuse to cut their hair in space, because Sasha Kaleri was cutting his hair when the fire started on *Mir*. I know as I hear the first peals of the alarm that I have set it off myself. I'm in the middle of cleaning an air filter and accidentally set free some dust that triggered the sensitive smoke detector. Still, an alarm is an alarm, and everyone has to respond according to the checklist. By the time it's resolved, I'm in a pretty crappy mood.

On Monday morning a couple of weeks later, it's time to work in the lab. Early in my career as an astronaut, I wasn't sure I even wanted to fly on the International Space Station. Most of what station astronauts do *is* science. I'm a pilot. My goal had been to pilot the hardest thing there was to fly: the space shuttle. Doing science experiments is a far cry from landing a space shuttle. But then again, so is unpacking cargo, repairing an air conditioner, or learning to speak Russian, and I do those things, too. I've come to appreciate that this job has challenged me to do not just one hard thing, but many hard things.

More than four hundred experiments will take place on ISS during this expedition, designed by scientists from many countries and representing many fields of study. Most of the experiments in one way or another study the effects of gravity—or the lack of gravity. Pretty much everything we know about the world around us is influenced by gravity. There are few branches of science that can't benefit from learning more about how gravity affects their subjects.

The research taking place on the station falls into two large categories. The first has to do with studies that might benefit life on Earth. The second has to do with solving problems for future space exploration. The study comparing Mark and me as twins over the course of the year falls into this second category. My sleep is being studied, as is my nutrition. My DNA will be analyzed to better understand the effects of spaceflight at a genetic level. Some of the studies being conducted on me are psychological and social: What are the effects of long-term isolation and confinement?

Science takes up about a third of my time, and studying myself and our crew takes up a huge part of that time. I must take blood samples from myself and my crewmates for analysis back on Earth, and I keep a log of everything from what I eat to my mood. I test my reaction skills at various points throughout the day. I take ultrasounds of blood vessels, my heart, my eyes, and my muscles. Later in this mission, I will take part in an experiment called Fluid Shifts, using a device that sucks the blood down to the lower half of my body, where gravity normally keeps it. This will test a leading theory about why spaceflight causes damage to some astronauts' vision.

Samantha working on a science experiment in the lab. July 2015.

At the end of the day, I head to my CQ and look through my care package that came up on Dragon again. There is a poem and some chocolates from Amiko (she knows I crave chocolate when I'm in space, though on Earth I don't have much of a sweet tooth); a bottle of Frank's hot sauce; a postcard from Mark showing twin redheaded little boys giving attitude to the camera; and a card from Charlotte and Samantha, their distinctive styles of handwriting gouged into the heavy paper by a black pen.

I eat a piece of the chocolate and put everything else away. I float in my sleeping bag for a while, thinking about my kids, wondering how they are doing with me being gone, until I drift off to sleep.

16

TODAY IS SATURDAY, almost two months into my mission.

Last night, April 25, we had movie night and watched *Gravity* with Sandra Bullock and George Clooney, about a disaster in space. We'd set up the big screen in Node 1 facing the lab and gathered to watch it—all of us except Samantha Cristoforetti, who was finishing her workout. I've noticed a strange phenomenon when people watch movies in space: we instinctually move to a position that looks like lying down in front of the screen. The association between lying down and relaxing is so strong that I actually feel more relaxed when I get into this position—even though it really makes no difference in zero g. The film was great—we were impressed by how real the ISS looked, and the five of us were an unusually tough audience in that regard. But it was a bit like watching a film of your own house burning while you're inside it.

The next night we have a birthday dinner for Samantha. Birthdays are important in Russian culture, too, and we make a point of celebrating them up here. This one is especially significant because soon Samantha, Terry, and Anton will be leaving us. As much as I will miss them all, I'm looking forward to breathing some good air (with half as many people exhaling, CO_2 levels will come down). I know the dropping CO_2 will likely cause the ground to act as though the problem has resolved itself, and I will be upset if that happens.

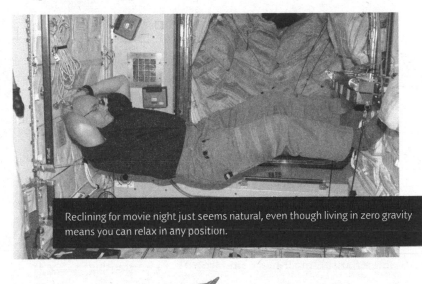

Reclining for movie night just seems natural, even though living in zero gravity means you can relax in any position.

Essential to getting to Mars, or anywhere else in space, is a working toilet, and ours does more than just store waste—our urine processor purifies our urine into drinking water. A system like this is necessary to interplanetary missions, since bringing thousands of gallons of drinking water to Mars simply wouldn't be possible. On the International Space Station, our urine processor distills our urine into water, which we drink, creating a nearly closed loop system. Some of that water we use to make our oxygen.

We are sent fresh water on resupply rockets, but we don't need it often. The Russians get fresh water from the Earth, which they drink and turn into pee, which they give to us to process into water. Cosmonaut urine is a hot commodity in an ongoing barter system of goods and services between the Russians and the Americans. They give us their pee; we share the electricity our solar cells have generated. They use their engines to reboost the station into the proper orbit; we help them when they are short on supplies.

Our urine processor, though, has been broken for about a week, so our urine is simply filling a holding tank. When it's full—it takes only a few days—a light will come on. In my experience, the light tends to turn on in the middle of the night. Replacing the tank is a pain, especially for a half-asleep handyman, but it's not an option to leave it for the morning. The first person to wake up won't be able to pee, which isn't good space station etiquette.

Now, in the light of day, I need to swap out the broken part. If everything goes right, the repair will take half the day. I've removed the "kabin" (the walls and the door) from the toilet in Node 3 so I can get at the machinery underneath. (The spelling comes from an error between Russian and English that stuck.) The kabin gets pretty gross, even though we try to clean it regularly. While I'm working on these repairs with the ground's assistance, another resupply rocket launched from Baikonur, a Russian Progress. My Russian crewmates on station followed the launch closely, getting updates from Russian mission control, and Anton floated down to let us know when it had reached orbit successfully. But now, less than ten minutes later, mission control in Moscow reports that a major malfunction has occurred and that the spacecraft is in a wild out-of-control spin. None of the workarounds they try correct the problem.

Up here, we talk about what it will mean for us if Progress is lost. We go over the supplies we have on board—food, clean clothes, oxygen, water, and replacement parts. Another resupply rocket exploded on the launchpad last October, this one built by the American company Orbital ATK, which means we are already behind on certain supplies. Each spacecraft brings different kinds of supplies, so even though the Dragon carried certain items we need, the loss of the Progress was still significant.

Misha, Gennady, and Anton keep us updated throughout the day, each time looking more and more concerned. Each of the cosmonauts had some personal items on board Progress, and sometimes those packages contain wedding rings and similar irreplaceable valuables.

As I'm working on our broken toilet, the ground tells us Progress has officially been declared lost. With a sinking feeling, I float over to the Russian segment to confer. Misha meets me in the service module, and it's clear he's heard the bad news.

"We'll give you guys anything you need," I say.

"Thank you, Scott," Misha says. I don't think I've ever seen such despair on another man's face. Losing Progress suddenly makes us realize how much we depend on a steady stream of successful resupply missions. We can afford one or two failures, but then we will have to start rationing.

Even more than our concern about supplies, though, is concern for our colleagues who will be launching soon: the rocket that doomed Progress is the same rocket that launches the manned Soyuz. Our three new crewmates, due up in a little less than a month, on May 26, are about to trust their lives to the same hardware and software. The Russian space agency must find out what went wrong and make sure it won't happen again. That will interfere with our schedule up here, but no one wants to fly on a Soyuz that's going to do the same thing this Progress did.

I finish making all the connections on the urine processor. Some of the cargo that was lost on Progress was fresh water, and unless we can make our own, the six of us won't last long. I double-check all the connections, then ask the ground to power it up. It works. The ground congratulates me, and I thank them for their help. It is satisfying knowing that we will be able to process urine and make clean water. I complete a few more maintenance tasks, make sure all the tools are put away properly, then run on the treadmill for half an hour.

While I'm running, a smoke alarm annunciates loudly. The treadmill under my feet stops automatically. The emergency signals are designed to get our attention, and they do. Even as I'm unhooking my running harness and scrambling to respond to the alarm, I'm pretty sure I know what caused it—as I was running I probably freed some dust from the treadmill or maybe caused the motor to smoke a bit by pushing against the treadmill in an effort to get my heart rate up. The fire alarm also automatically shuts down ventilation in Node 3, and that shuts down our Seedra. After we're fully recovered from the alarm, the ground informs us that they can't restart the Seedra and aren't sure why. I'm less than thrilled by the prospect of rising CO_2 until we can get it running again.

Because the next Soyuz launch is delayed until the problem is figured out, that means Terry, Samantha, and Anton will be delayed in their return as well. I know this must be stressful for them—we each know how long we'll be here and pace ourselves. I can't imagine having to tell my family I'm not coming back when I'd said I would, and that I have no idea when I will return. Outwardly, my crewmates all appear professional and upbeat.

Still no word from the Russians on why the Progress

malfunctioned. We don't know whether they have a good the-ory and just haven't confirmed it or if they actually have no clue whatsoever. Terry, Anton, and Samantha still don't know what their landing date will be. Every afternoon, Terry floats over to the Russian segment to ask Anton whether he has heard anything new about the Soyuz return. According to Terry, Anton shrugs and says no. Then Gennady tells us Moscow has identi-fied a possible culprit for the Progress failure. He also tells us that our Soyuz, the one we came up here in and that Gennady will take back down with two other people in September, might have the same issue. Not good news.

Since the ground was never able to get the Node 3 Seedra working again after the fire alarm, Terry and I are working to-gether to repair it. It's a complicated, absorbing, detailed job—but our lives just happen to depend on it. The other Seedra isn't working right either, which puts a lot of pressure on us to make sure we fix this one.

It's unbelievable how much of a pain this thing is—even with Terry's help. It takes half an hour just to remove one bolt, and Terry tears up the back of his hand so much in the process he has to bandage it. After a break to eat lunch, we return and finish the job. As we are putting our tools away, Terry shouts something with a childlike excitement in his voice: "Hey! Candy!"

A little piece of something edible looking is floating by. It often happens that bits of food get away from us and provide an unexpected snack for someone days later.

I warn him, "It might not be chocolate."

He takes a closer look at it. "It's a used Band-Aid," he says. He catches it and puts it in the trash. Later that night, we tell

Samantha the story and she tells us that last week *she* ate something she thought was candy and realized only too late that it was garbage.

In the next morning's daily planning conference, we learn that Terry, Samantha, and Anton will leave on June 11, more than a month late. Their Soyuz has been docked here since November, and it's only safe for the spacecraft to sit idle for a certain period of time. It's not clear how much of this decision hinges on that ticking time clock, and how much is a sign of their confidence the Soyuz is free of the issues that doomed Progress. Either way, the Russian space agency has weighed the risks and decided it will soon be time for them to go. And the new crew will come up on July 22. I will be alone for six weeks on the U.S. segment before their replacements arrive. It's a long time to be floating around by myself, but being alone doesn't seem like a bad thing. I like having crewmates, and I've especially enjoyed working with Terry and Samantha, but being alone won't be an unwelcome change. Besides, each time people leave or arrive marks another milestone of my mission that I've successfully put behind me.

The International Space Station is orbiting fast enough that the force of gravity keeps it curving around the Earth. We think of objects in orbit as being stable, staying at the same distance above the planet, but in reality, the Earth's surface pulls on us even when we are whizzing along at 17,500 miles per hour. Without help, our orbit would tighten until we eventually crashed into the planet's surface.

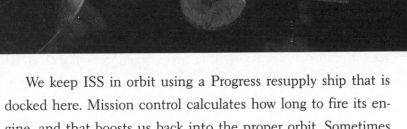

This docked Soyuz has been waiting longer than usual to bring Terry, Samantha, and Anton home. April 29, 2015.

We keep ISS in orbit using a Progress resupply ship that is docked here. Mission control calculates how long to fire its engine, and that boosts us back into the proper orbit. Sometimes we wake up in the morning to learn that a successful reboost has taken place while we slept.

This morning, though, an attempted reboost failed. Once again, a Progress has failed to function properly, and once again, we must worry about what that will mean for us.

We are not in any immediate danger of crashing into the Earth—it would take many months for our orbit to decay to a dangerous degree—but we also use the Progress engines to move the station out of the way of all the stuff in orbit around the

Earth—satellites, still working or not, and pieces of satellites that were blown apart in orbital collisions—so the failure could have frightening consequences.

That Friday night, we are having dinner on the Russian segment, and we know it will be one of our last with Terry, Anton, and Samantha. Terry floats to the U.S. segment to get the last of the ice cream that came up on Dragon, and when he comes back, he has a troubled look on his face.

"Scott, the ground is trying to get in touch with you," he says. "You need to call your daughter Samantha right away. They said it's an emergency."

My crewmates all look at me with concern. They know that I got a similar call on the space station five years ago, when my sister-in-law was shot.

"I'm sure it's nothing," I say, for their benefit more than mine. I go to my CQ, where I can talk privately. Only then do I realize that we don't have satellite coverage in our current location, and I won't be able to make a call for twenty minutes. This is one of my most terrifying moments from my year in space, worrying about what could have happened to my daughter. I spend that time thinking about Samantha, about what she was like as a spirited toddler, as a bright-eyed school-age kid, as a moody teenager. I know that Samantha has had to deal with fallout from the divorce, caring for her mother and her younger sister in ways that I don't even know about. It's been an ongoing struggle to get to a place where we can be comfortable with each other without fear of blowups.

When the communication satellites are finally aligned, I put on my headset and click on the icon to place a call to Samantha's cell. She answers on the second ring.

"Hi, Dad." She knows it's me because calls from the space station are all routed through the Johnson Space Center.

"Are you okay? What's going on?" I ask, trying to sound calm.

"Not much," she says. "I'm at Uncle Mark and Gabby's. Everyone has left, and I'm lonely." I can tell from her tone that nothing serious is wrong. She sounds bored.

"That's it? There's no emergency?" I ask, feeling my concern give way to irritation. It felt like the times I'd lost track of one of the girls at a shopping center and looked for them long enough to start fearing the worst.

Samantha explains that she flew to Tucson for the high school graduation of her cousin Claire, Mark's younger daughter. Samantha has been going through a hard time and was feeling cut off from our family while I am away. So she thought it might make her feel better to be at a gathering of Kellys. But the night after the graduation, Mark and Gabby left town, and shortly after that, Claudia, Mark's older daughter, left as well, leaving Samantha by herself in an empty house. She felt abandoned and wanted to get home. She tried emailing me, but when she didn't hear back, she called Mike Fincke, an astronaut classmate of mine. When he conveyed her request to mission control, her request was misinterpreted as an emergency.

The absurdity is not lost on me that *I'm* in space for a year, and she's lonely. But I'm also reminded just how much my family is sacrificing for this mission.

She apologizes for scaring me and promises to leave a clearer message next time. I go back over to the Russian segment to rejoin the festivities, my mood somewhat dampened.

17

WE WILL BE spending a lot of time this week working on an experiment called "Fluid Shifts Before, During, and After Prolonged Space Flight and Their Association with Intracranial Pressure and Visual Impairment"—"Fluid Shifts" for short. Misha and I are the subjects of the experiment, and it promises some of the most important results for the future of spaceflight.

Maybe the most troubling negative effect of long-duration missions in space has been damage to astronauts' vision, including mine on my previous mission. At first, these changes were assumed to be temporary. Once astronauts started flying longer and longer missions, though, we showed more severe symptoms. For most, the changes gradually disappeared once the mission was over, but for some, the symptoms seemed to be permanent.

During my first long-duration flight, 159 days, my vision got worse. When I returned to Earth, within a few months my vision returned to what it had been when I left. But I had other troubling signs, like the swelling of the optic nerve. My vision symptoms so far this year seem to be similar to the last time, though we are watching closely to see whether they will get worse.

If long-term spaceflight could do serious damage to astronauts' vision, this is one of the problems that must be solved before we can get to Mars. You can't have a crew attempting to land on a faraway planet—piloting the spacecraft, operating complex hardware, and exploring the surface—if they can't see well.

The leading hypothesis is that increased pressure in the cerebral fluid surrounding our brains is causing the vision changes. In space, we don't have gravity to pull blood and other fluids to the lower half of our bodies. So the cerebral fluid does not drain properly and tends to increase the pressure in our heads. We adjust over the first few weeks in space and pee away a lot of the excess, but the full-head sensation never completely goes away. It feels a little like standing on your head twenty-four hours a day—mild pressure in your ears, congestion, round face, flushed skin.

The increased fluid pressure may squish our eyeballs out of shape and cause swelling in the blood vessels of our eyes and optic nerves. This is all still a theory, as it's hard to measure the pressure inside our skulls in space.

It's possible, too, that high CO_2, which is known to widen blood vessels, is causing or contributing to changes in our vision. High sodium in our space diets could also be a factor, and NASA has been working to reduce that in order to test whether this makes a difference. Only male astronauts have suffered damage to their eyes while in space, so looking at the slight differences in the head and neck veins of male and female astronauts might also help scientists start to nail down the causes. If we can't, we just might have to send an all-women crew to Mars.

In the Fluid Shifts study, Misha and I will be subjects in an experiment that uses a device for relieving the pressure in our heads from spaceflight—pants that suck. This is not a metaphor. We will take turns wearing a device, roughly the shape of a pair of pants, called Chibis (Russian for "lapwing," a type of bird), that reduces the pressure on the lower half of our bodies. The pants look a lot like the bottom half of the robot from *Lost in Space*, or like Wallace and Gromit's "wrong trousers." By studying the effects of Chibis pants on our bodies, we hope to understand more about this problem.

One of the times these pants were used, however, the Russian cosmonaut wearing them experienced a sudden drop in heart rate and lost consciousness. His crewmates thought he was having a heart attack and immediately ended the experiment without causing any permanent physical damage. Anytime a piece of equipment has put a person at risk, NASA has been reluctant to use it again. But because the Chibis pants are still the best possibility we have for understanding this problem, they are making an exception.

Preparing to put on the "pants" is actually a days-long process. We have to take samples of blood, saliva, and urine before the test, and images of blood vessels in our heads, necks, and eyes using ultrasound. Then we can compare them to results of the same tests during the experiment. This is going to be the most complicated human experiment that's ever been done on the International Space Station.

When it's time to put on the device, I take off my pants and clamber into the Chibis pants, making sure the seal around my waist is secure. Misha is working the controls, slowly decreasing the pressure on my lower body. With each small change, I can feel the blood being pulled out of my head—in a good way. For the first time in months, I don't feel like I'm standing on my head.

But then the feeling starts to change. It's like I'm in an F-14 jet again, pulling too many g's. I can feel myself starting to gray

Me wearing the Chibis during the Fluid Shifts study. September 2015.

out, feeling at risk of passing out. The pants are malfunctioning, and I feel like I could have my intestines pulled out in the most unpleasant way possible.

"Hey, something's not right with this," I announce to Misha and Gennady. "I'm gonna have to—" I reach for the seal at my waist, prepared to break it, canceling the experiment. At the same instant, I hear Gennady yelling.

"Misha, *shto ty delayesh?*" What are you doing? Gennady doesn't yell much, so when he raises his voice, you can be sure you have likely screwed up. In this case, I look over at the pressure gauge, which is not supposed to go past 55. Misha has it down to 80, the maximum negative pressure.

Fortunately, neither I nor the equipment sustains any permanent damage, and we are able to go on with the experiment. I stay in the pants for a couple of hours, doing all the needed tests. This is where my space tattoos come in handy. Shortly before my launch, I visited a Houston tattoo parlor and had some black dots placed on the most-used ultrasound sites (on my neck, biceps, thigh, and calf) so I could easily find the exact spot each time. It's saved me a huge amount of trouble already. We measure my ear and eye pressure. We scan my eyeball with a laser, which can show changes like choroidal folds and optic nerve swelling.

During the time we're doing this, I feel as good as I've ever felt in space. The constant pressure in my head clears, and I'm sorry when it's time to shed the pants and shut the experiment down.

Later in the day, I'm sitting on the toilet in the Waste and Hygiene Compartment. Samantha is brushing her teeth just outside the kabin, which is like a stall in a public restroom—and I can hear her humming to herself, as she often does while she works.

I can see her socked feet under the wall, hooked under a handrail to keep her steady. Her toes are close enough that I could reach out and tickle them, but I decide against it.

This scene probably sounds a bit odd to those who haven't experienced the loss of privacy on a space station, but we get used to it. I've just been reading about how the men on the Shackleton expedition had to hunker down behind snowdrifts and had only chunks of ice to clean themselves with, so I count myself lucky. Because I have nothing else to do while I sit on the toilet, I watch Samantha's feet hooked under the handrail, keeping her body perfectly still, and I think about the complexity of that simple task. If you showed me nothing but a foot hooked under a handrail in zero gravity, I could estimate how long that person has been in space with a high degree of accuracy. When Samantha was new up here, she would have hooked her feet too hard, used too much force, and tired out her ankles and big toe joints unnecessarily. Now she knows exactly how little pressure she needs to apply. Her toes move with the elegance and precision of a pianist's fingers on a keyboard.

Last night we enjoyed our final Friday dinner with Terry, Samantha, and Anton. Since the loss of the Progress, the Russians are running low on food and other supplies, and though we've made it clear we will share food, things won't be the same for a while. I bring over a salami my brother sent up on the last Dragon, and I eat some of the last of the Russian meals, a "Can of White" (chicken with white sauce), and some American "Bags of Brown" (some sort of irradiated beef thing). The Russians also have something called "the Appetizing Appetizer," which it is not.

A few of us say we have been craving fruit recently, which is no surprise given that there has been no fresh food in our diets since shortly after Dragon arrived, which seems like months ago. Our dried, bagged, and canned fruits are not the same as the real deal. When the next Dragon resupply gets here at the end of June, it will finally bring fresh fruits and vegetables as well as desperately needed supplies, chief among them the poop cans that store our solid waste, which are so vital to life in space. My brother has also announced he is sending me a gorilla suit on Dragon. I asked why I needed a gorilla suit on the space station.

"Of course you need a gorilla suit," he responded. "You're getting a gorilla suit. There's no stopping me."

On Wednesday, June 11, the day before the Soyuz is to leave, Terry must hand over command of the station to Gennady. There's a little ceremony, a military tradition drawn from the Navy change-of-command ceremony, that lets everyone know clearly when responsibility for the station transfers from one person to another. The six of us float somewhat awkwardly in the U.S. lab while Terry makes a speech. He thanks the ground teams in Houston, Moscow, Japan, Europe, and Canada, as well as the science support teams in Huntsville and other places. He thanks our families for supporting us on our missions.

"So now Expedition Forty-Three is in the history books, and we turn it over to a new chapter and Expedition Forty-Four." With that, he hands the microphone to Gennady, who checks to see if it is still on.

"No matter how many flights you have," Gennady says, "it's always like a new station, always like first flight."

This makes everyone smile, because Gennady has more spaceflights than any of us (this is his fifth), and he will soon set a record for most days in space of any human. Gennady wishes Terry, Anton, and Samantha a "soft, safe landing and the best return home." Terry tells the control center that this concludes the handover ceremony, and another milestone of my mission is crossed off. The next handover ceremony will be in September, when Gennady leaves and I become commander.

Later that night, Terry asks me what landing is like in the Soyuz. He's trained for this, of course, and he has been told what to expect by Anton and by the training team at Star City; still, he is curious to hear my experience. I think of how to set him up for what to expect without scaring him too much.

We call Samantha over so she can hear it, too, and I describe what my experience had been last time: as we slammed into the atmosphere, the capsule was engulfed in a bright orange plasma, which is a little disconcerting, sort of like having your face a few inches away from a window while on the other side someone is trying to get at you with a blowtorch. Then, when the parachute deployed, the capsule spun and twisted and turned violently in every direction. If you can get in the right frame of mind, if you can experience it like an adventure ride, this can be great fun. On the other hand, some astronauts and cosmonauts, after their first Soyuz landing, have said that they were being thrown around so violently they became convinced something had gone wrong and they were going to die. There can be a fine line between terror and fun, and I want to give Terry and Samantha the right mind-set.

Terry has experienced the ride back to Earth on the space shuttle, and I tell him the Soyuz reentry is much steeper. "The shuttle reentry feels like cruising down Park Avenue in a Rolls-Royce," I tell him. "Riding the Soyuz is more like riding an old Soviet junk car down an unpaved street that leads off a cliff."

They both think this analogy is funny, but they also appear a little worried.

"As soon as you realize you aren't going to die, it's the most fun you'll ever have," I tell them. "I'll tell you the truth—the ride is so much fun, I would sign up for another long-duration mission just to get to take that ride again." Terry and Samantha look skeptical, but it's true.

Our crewmates are leaving today. There is a ceremony for the hatch closing, seen live on NASA TV, as they depart. It starts out a bit awkwardly, since all six of us are crammed into the narrow Russian module where their Soyuz is docked. I snap some pictures of Anton, Samantha, and Terry posing in the open hatch. Then those who are staying wish them good luck and a soft landing. There are lots of hugs, and then the three of them float into the Soyuz and give one last wave while we take their pictures.

Anton and Gennady wipe down the hatch seal in the vestibule, to make sure that no foreign objects keep the hatch from sealing properly. Gennady closes the hatch on our side while Anton is closing it from their side. And that's it. It's a weird thing: I've spent so much time with these people, but with a few good-byes and hugs, our shared experience is over in an instant.

I'm not scared for my departing crewmates, any more than I'm scared for myself, but seeing the hatch close behind them gives me a strange sense of isolation, even abandonment. If I have to work on the Seedra again, I'll have to do it without Terry's help. If

I get into a discussion with the Russians about literature, I'll have to do it without Samantha's help. I'm looking forward to having the U.S. segment to myself, though, and I try to focus on that.

I float off toward the U.S. lab. "Catch up with you later," I say to my Russian colleagues, and they float off to their segment, then all is silent. It's just me and the fan noise.

Then I hear Terry's voice, breaking in mid-sentence, as if he were here with me: ". . . pills for the fluid loading protocol, Anton? Or did you leave them on station?"

"I've got them," Anton answers, then rattles off a series of numbers in rapid-fire Russian to their control center. Now that the communications on the Soyuz are set up, I can hear through our intercom system every word my former crewmates say as if I were in there with them. I go through the rest of the afternoon listening to Terry's, Anton's, and Samantha's voices.

When the Soyuz is ready to detach and push away from station, three hours after we closed the hatch, I watch its departure on a laptop screen on NASA TV, just as many people on Earth are doing. I grab a mic.

"Fair winds and following seas, guys," I say, a U.S. Navy phrase used when friends and crewmates depart. "It was a real pleasure spending time up here with you, and good luck on your landing."

Terry answers, "Thanks, Scott, we miss you guys already."

Gennady adds from the Russian segment, "Samantha, I think you forgot your sweater," joking about the blue sweater she often wore throughout her time on board.

I hear them talking to one another this way, trading idle work chat and calling out numbers to ground control, almost all the way to the ground. If I didn't know what they were doing—falling like a meteor at supersonic speed toward the planet's surface—I could never have guessed.

The Soyuz capsule carrying Terry, Samantha, and Anton made a flaming return to Earth. June 11, 2015.

Several hours later, they are on the ground safely in Kazakhstan. They had been here with me twenty-four hours a day for months, and now they are as far and unreachable as everyone else on Earth, as Amiko and my daughters and the 7 billion other humans.

That night, when I turn out the lights and climb into my sleeping bag, I'm aware of the quiet. There is no rustling in the other crew quarters or quiet talking as crewmates communicate with the ground or say good night to their families on the phone. If this were a normal six-month flight, I would already be halfway done, but instead I feel I have as long as I did when I first got up here. Nine months. I don't often let these kinds of thoughts into my head, but when I do it's hard to get them out again. What have I gotten myself into?

Sunday rarely feels like a Sunday on the space station, but today might be an exception. Yesterday I did both my weekly cleaning and my exercise, so today I actually have the entire day off. When I wake, I read the daily summary that was sent to us overnight and see that today Gennady sets the world record for the most total days in space: 803. By the time he leaves, he will have 879, a record I expect to stand for a long time.

There is a SpaceX launch scheduled today for 2:20 p.m. our time (10:20 a.m. in Florida). SpaceX is carrying a lot of things we are looking forward to getting:

- food (the Russians are still running low)
- water
- clothing for American astronaut Kjell (pronounced "Chell") Lindgren and Japanese astronaut Kimiya Yui, who will both arrive next month
- spacewalk equipment for Kjell, who will be my spacewalking partner in the fall
- filtration beds for removing contaminants from our water (which is close to undrinkable, since the last set of beds blew up on Orbital)
- experiments designed by schoolchildren (some of the kids who saw their experiments blow up are being given a second chance to see their work go to space today)

Personally, I'm looking forward to an extra set of running shoes, another harness for the treadmill, clean clothes, and crew care packages that my friends and family chose for me.

Launch time comes and goes. Shortly after, I look up the video for the SpaceX launch on my laptop. Then my eye stops on a headline: "SpaceX Rocket Explodes During Cargo Launch to Space Station."

You've got to be kidding me.

The flight director gets on a privatized space-to-ground channel and tells us the rocket has been lost.

"Station copies," I say.

I take a moment to think over all the stuff that has been lost. All blown to bits. I joke to Mark that the thing I'm saddest about is the gorilla suit. After having to be talked into it, I had started thinking about all the fun Space Gorilla could have up here. Now he is a burned cinder, like everything else on the spacecraft. As stunned as I am by the loss, I am overwhelmed by what this will mean for the rest of my year in space and beyond. It starts to sink in that we have lost three resupply vehicles in the last nine months, the last two in a row. Our supplies are now down to about three months' worth, and the Russians are much worse off than that.

I think about the schoolchildren who saw their experiments blow up on Orbital, rebuilt them, and saw them blow up on SpaceX. I hope they will get a third chance. There is a lesson here, I guess, about risk and resilience, about endurance and trying again.

18

BEING ALONE IN the U.S. segment, I can go all day without seeing another person, unless I have reason to visit my Russian colleagues. I appreciate the quiet and the privacy, a rare luxury up here. I can blast music or enjoy uninterrupted silence. I keep CNN on all day, at least when the satellites are lined up, for some company.

I do sometimes miss having another person to talk to, even if it's just to complain about the challenging work schedule or to talk about what's on the news. And I miss being able to get a bit of help now and then. My workdays are longer when I do everything alone. The cosmonauts would drop everything to help if I needed them to, but they have their own work.

I wake up early in the morning, six a.m., and float out of my CQ, through the lab and Node 1, turning on lights as I go. I turn right, into Node 3, where I go into the WHC, the space toilet. I don't start it up, though—today is a science sample collection day. The process of peeing is going to be even more complicated than usual—let me spare you all the dirty details. After I finish peeing, I head down to the Japanese module to put the tubes of pee I collected into one of the freezers. I will do this every time I urinate for the next twenty-four hours.

With the pee sample done, I head into the European Columbus module for my blood draw. Like most astronauts on ISS, I know how to draw my own blood. But today, Gennady joins me in Columbus to help.

After cleaning the site on my left arm, he grabs a butterfly needle and connects it to the tube holder. Then he takes aim and slides the needle perfectly into my vein. But the needle isn't properly connected to the tube holder, so blood escapes, flowing out into globs that wobble and then form into crimson spheres, traveling in every direction. Gennady quickly fixes the connection while I reach out to grab some of the blood spheres with my hand before they can float farther away. The ones I missed I'll have to track down and clean up later.

Gennady changes out the tubes over and over until he's drawn ten tubes of blood. I thank him for his help, and he goes back to the service module to have breakfast. After I process the tubes, I put them in the freezer along with the other samples.

Later in the day, I will take a feces sample; tomorrow, saliva and skin. I will go through this whole test process every few weeks for the rest of the year.

The CO_2 is much better now that I'm the only one exhaling on this side of the ISS. My headaches and congestion have largely cleared up, and I notice a difference in my mood and clearer thought processes. I'm appreciating this break from the symptoms while I can. Soon, the next crew will get here and we will start the whole cycle all over again.

One of the nice things about living in space is that exercise is part of your job, not something you have to fit in before or after work. (Of course, that's also one of the bad things about it: there are no excuses.) If I don't exercise six days a week for at least a couple of hours a day, my bones will lose significant mass—1 percent each month. We've had two astronauts break their hips after long-duration spaceflights. And since the risk of death after hip fracture increases with age, bone loss is one of the biggest dangers my year in space will pose to my future health. Even with all this exercise, I will lose some bone mass, and it's suspected that bone structure changes permanently after long-term spaceflight (this is one of the many medical questions Misha's and my year will help to answer). Our bodies are smart about getting rid of what's not needed, and my body has started to notice that my bones are not needed in zero gravity. Not having to support our weight, we lose muscle as well.

When it's workout time on my schedule, I float into the Permanent Multipurpose Module (PMM), a windowless module we use as a large closet, to change into shorts, socks, and a shirt. The PMM always reminds me of my grandparents' basement—it's dark, dingy, and has random stuff everywhere. My workout clothes are getting a bit smelly because I've been using them for a couple of weeks. There is no laundry up here, so we wear clothes for as long as we can stand, then throw them out. I struggle to find something to hook my feet onto while I change.

I head into Node 3 and make my way to the treadmill. On the ceiling is a strap that holds a pair of shoes, a harness, and a heart monitor for each of us. I grab my running shoes and put them on; then I step onto the treadmill, which is mounted on the "wall."

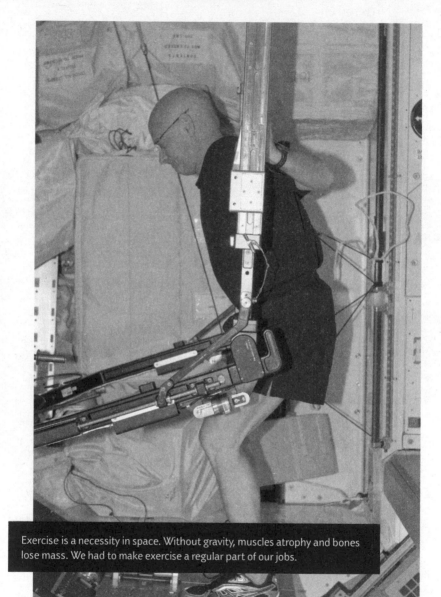

Exercise is a necessity in space. Without gravity, muscles atrophy and bones lose mass. We had to make exercise a regular part of our jobs.

I put my harness on, buckle it at the waist and chest, and clip into the bungee system that's attached to the treadmill. This holds me in place as I run—without the harness, I would go flying off the treadmill with my first step. I set up the laptop in front of me and start an episode of *Game of Thrones*. I'm watching the whole series for the second time.

In some ways, our treadmill is like the one you might find in a gym on Earth, but it's mounted into its own unique vibration isolation system. The forces created by the runner pounding away could be surprisingly dangerous—vibrating at the wrong frequency could actually tear the space station apart. On *Mir*, Russian mission control once had to ask American astronaut Shannon Lucid to run at a different pace or risk damaging the space station.

While I'm running, Gennady comes floating by. It's hard to sneak by the person on the treadmill without distracting them or, worse, hitting or kicking them, especially for people who are new on station. It takes some getting used to, seeing someone running on the wall.

Gennady is here to check out some poop cans temporarily stored in a big bag on the floor of Node 1, waiting to go out on the outgoing Progress with the rest of the garbage, and he'd noticed they were smelling a bit. He checks one of the lids to make sure it's sealed properly, only to accidentally free a cloud of toxic gas that nearly knocks me off the treadmill. The entire U.S. segment smells wretched for a while, but I'm impressed by how quickly the system filters the air.

"As soon as I get back to Earth," Gennady mutters in Russian, "I am going on a vacation."

Soon after he leaves, I hear the voice of mission control.

"Station, Houston on Space to Ground Two. We are privatizing the space-to-ground channel. The flight director needs to speak to you."

We are privatizing. These are words that make any astronaut's blood freeze. I bring the treadmill to a stop, unhook myself, and grab the mic to talk to Houston.

I hear the capcom on duty, Jay Marschke, refer to the trajectory operations officer (TOPO). For a moment, I'm relieved; at least it has nothing to do with my family.

"This is a red late-notice conjunction," Jay says, "with a closest point of approach within a sphere of uncertainty."

"Roger," I say into the microphone. I try to sound calm, though inside I'm immediately on red alert.

A "conjunction" is a potential collision—a piece of space junk is headed our way, in this case an old Russian satellite. "Late notice" means we didn't see it coming or that we miscalculated its path, and "red" means it's going to get dangerously close—we just don't know how close. The "sphere of uncertainty" refers to the area it could pass through, a sphere with a radius of one mile. Because the impact could let our air out and kill us all, we will have to head to the Soyuz and use it as a possible lifeboat. If the debris streaking toward us collides with us, we will likely all be dead in two hours.

"How about relative velocity?" I ask. "Any idea?"

"Closing velocity of fourteen kilometers per second," comes the answer.

"Copy," I say into my headset. This is the worst possible answer to my question. The space station is traveling in one direction at 17,500 miles per hour, and the space junk is traveling just as fast in the opposite direction—twenty times faster than a bullet from a rifle. If the satellite hits, the resulting destruction would be like a nuclear explosion.

With six hours' notice, the space station can move itself out of the way of oncoming orbital debris. The Air Force tracks the position and trajectory of thousands of objects in orbit—mostly old satellites, whole or in chunks. As with everything else, NASA has an abbreviation for these adjustments: PDAM, or predetermined debris avoidance maneuvers, which means firing the station's engines to get us out of the way. We've had two PDAMs since I've been up here. Today, however, is different. With only two hours' notice, a PDAM will not be possible.

Mission control directs me to close and check all the hatches on the U.S. segment of the space station. I trained to do this in my preparations for this mission, and I run through the checklist in my mind in order to complete the steps properly and—most important—quickly. With the hatches closed, if one module is hit, the others might survive—or at least their contents won't be sucked out into the vacuum of space. There are eighteen hatches on the U.S. segment that must be closed or checked. While I'm working, I get a call from mission control.

"Scott, Misha, it's time to get ready for your event with WDRB in Louisville, Kentucky."

"What?" I ask, incredulous. "Is there really time to be doing this?"

Misha shows up in the U.S. lab for our joint public affairs event, as he always does, with no time to spare but right on time.

"Public affairs events can't be canceled," comes the answer. This is insane.

"Are they kidding?" I say to Misha. He shakes his head in response. This is a bad decision, but it's also not a great time to get into an argument with the ground.

Misha and I get into position in front of the camera with the handheld microphone.

"Station, Houston, are you ready for the event?" Jay asks.

"We are ready for the event," I answer, struggling to keep the annoyance out of my voice. We spend the next five minutes answering questions about what we think of the probe that just reached Pluto, what landmark we may be passing over, and whether we got to watch the Kentucky Derby back in May. When we are asked about maneuvering in weightlessness, we turn somersaults for the Louisville viewers before signing off, still feeling upset that we had to waste our time this way, given the jeopardy we are in. There is danger in taking the safety of life on an orbiting space station for granted, and the decision to go ahead with this interview is, to me, clearly a symptom of that.

Misha and I do a public presentation in July 2015, as we did on the day space debris almost obliterated the ISS.

As soon as the cameras are off, I get back to checking that the hatches are closed. I collect the items from the U.S. segment that we will need most if a collision destroys that part of the station: the defibrillator, the advanced life support medical kit, my iPad with important procedures on it, my iPod, and a bag of personal items. By the time I have gathered all my important items, we have about twenty minutes to spare before potential impact.

I go to the Russian segment, where I see that the cosmonauts have not bothered with closing their hatches. They think closing the hatches is a waste of time, and they have a point. The two most likely scenarios are that the satellite will miss us, in which case closing the hatches will have been pointless, or it will hit us, in which case the station will be vaporized in an instant, and it won't make a bit of difference if the hatches are open or closed. It is incredibly unlikely that one module could be hit and the others survive intact, but just in case, mission control has me spend more than two hours preparing. The Russian approach is to say "whatever" and spend what might be their last twenty minutes having lunch. I reach my crewmates in time to join them for a small can of Appetizing Appetizer.

Ten minutes before potential impact, we make our way to the Soyuz, which Gennady has prepared for flight in case we have to detach from the station. It's orbital night now and dark in the Soyuz as we each slide into our seats. It's cramped and cold and loud.

"You know," Gennady says, "it will really stink if we get hit by this satellite."

"*Da,*" Misha agrees. "Will stink."

Only four other times in the history of the ISS have crews had to shelter in place as we are now. I can hear our breathing over the sounds of the fans stirring the air inside the Soyuz. I don't think any one of us is actually fearful. We've all been in risky situations before. We do talk, though, about the size and speed of the piece of space junk coming toward us. We all agree that it's a potentially disastrous scenario.

Misha stares out the window. I remind him that he won't be able to see the satellite coming toward us—it will be going way too fast for the human eye to see it. And besides, it's dark outside. He keeps looking anyway, and soon I'm looking out my window, too. The clock counts down. Once the time gets down to seconds, I feel myself tensing, starting to grimace. We wait. Then . . . nothing. Thirty seconds go by. We look at one another with a last heartbeat of anticipation of disaster. Then our grimaces slowly turn into expressions of relief.

"Moscow, are we still waiting?" Gennady asks.

"Gennady Ivanovich, that's it," Moscow mission control responds. "The moment has passed. It is safe; you can go back to work now."

We float out of the Soyuz one by one, Gennady and Misha finish lunch, and then I spend most of the day opening all the hatches.

Later, as I reflect on the situation, I realize that if the satellite had in fact hit us, we probably wouldn't even have known it. Misha, Gennady, and I would have gone from grumbling to one another in our cold Soyuz to being blasted in a million directions as diffused atoms, all in the space of a millisecond. Our brains would not even have had time to process the incoming data into conscious thought.

I don't know whether this comforts me or disturbs me.

19

ON JULY 22, the Expedition 44 crew arrived. My six weeks of solitude in the U.S. module are over. Their launch and docking went off without a hitch, which was a relief after the recent Progress failures. When we opened the hatch and the new guys came floating through, looking dazed as baby birds right out of the shell, I was reminded of the day I passed through the same hatch in my Captain America suit, Misha and me fitting through the opening together like a set of conjoined twins. It feels like that was years ago. The days are going by quickly, but the weeks crawl. Kjell, Kimiya, and Oleg's arrival marks the passage of only one-third of my time here.

The three new guys will need a lot of help getting used to zero g and learning to work in this environment. For experienced astronauts serving on ISS for the first time, the adjustment period is longer than for those who have lived here before; for first-time space travelers, like Kjell Lindgren and Kimiya Yui, it's longer still. (This is Oleg Kononenko's third time in space.)

More than two-thirds of space travelers suffer from some degree of space motion sickness, and there isn't much to be done but wait it out. Kjell and Kimiya both feel pretty bad on day one. Until they fully adapt, they will be as clumsy and tentative as babies just learning to walk. They will need help with the simplest things; even moving from one module to another without knocking things off the walls is a challenge. They will need help talking to the ground, preparing food, using the bathroom. Even the process of throwing up requires help initially. It will take them four to six weeks to feel fully adjusted.

Kjell has a great attitude so far and seems enthusiastic about everything he approaches, even though he looks a bit pale, with dark circles under his eyes. Every once in a while, he gets a distracted look, then excuses himself to throw up. The first few days in space can make anyone cranky, but Kjell doesn't seem to have forgotten for one second that he is living his boyhood dream, and his positive attitude is contagious.

Kimiya is one of seven active Japanese astronauts (there are approximately forty-five active American astronauts, approximately thirty Russian, and sixteen representing the European Space Agency). When I first got to know him in training, he seemed very formal. He would call me "Kelly-san," a formal (though not the most formal) way to address another person in Japan. When I kept trying to get him to just call me "Scott," he started calling me "Scott-san." Kimiya understands that Americans value informality and equality—at least in our interactions—and he tries to meet us halfway.

Oleg Kononenko is a seasoned cosmonaut and a brilliant engineer. He is a quiet and thoughtful person, consistently reliable. He is the same age as me and has a pair of twins the same age as Charlotte, a boy and a girl.

Kjell and Kimiya are growing used to the strangely sterile life up here. At least now we have some plants: we have begun an experiment in the European module growing lettuce. We are learning more about the challenges of growing food in space, which will be important if humans are to make a journey to Mars.

I recently noticed that my brain has made a transition to living in zero g—I can now see things in all directions. If I'm "upside down," instead of the environment looking foreign and disorienting, as it would if you stood on your head in an equipment-packed laboratory on Earth, now I immediately recognize where I am and can find whatever I need. This is a transition I never made last time, even after 159 days in space.

I've been noticing that Misha has a different philosophy of pacing himself through the year than I do—he often announces the exact number of days we still have to go, which kind of drives me nuts. I prefer to count up rather than count down, as if the days are something valuable I'm collecting.

I decided to kick off the month of August with a Twitter chat, answering questions from followers "live." I'm answering the usual questions about food, exercise, and the view of Earth when I receive a tweet from a user with the handle @POTUS44, President Obama.

He writes, "Hey @StationCDRKelly, loving the photos. Do you ever look out the window and just freak out?"

I think for a moment, then reply: "I don't freak out about anything, Mr. President, except getting a Twitter question from you."

It's a great Twitter moment, unplanned and unscripted, and it gets thousands of likes and retweets. Not long after, a reply appears from Buzz Aldrin: "He's 249 miles above the earth. Piece of cake. Neil, Mike & I went 239,000 miles to the moon. #Apollo11."

There is no good way to engage in a Twitter debate with an American hero, so I don't. In my mind, I reflect on the fact that the crew of Apollo 11 spent eight days in space, traveling half a million miles; by the time I'm done, I will have spent a total of 520 days in space and will have traveled over two hundred million miles, the equivalent of going to Mars and back. Only later, when the Twitter chat is over, do I have the chance to think that I just experienced being trolled, in space, by the second man on the moon, while also engaging in a Twitter conversation with the president.

A few days later, it's time to harvest the lettuce we've been growing. Kjell, Kimiya, and I gather in the European module to eat it with some oil and vinegar, and it's surprisingly good. This is the first time American astronauts have eaten a crop grown in space, though the Russians have grown and eaten leafy greens on previous missions. As often happens, the public reaction to the space lettuce surprises me—people seem to be fascinated by the idea of growing and eating plants in orbit, while at the same time Misha and Gennady are outside doing a spacewalk that gets no attention in the United States whatsoever.

That evening, we bring the Russians some lettuce to sample for Friday dinner. The main topic of discussion is the Soyuz that will be coming up soon, bringing our total to nine. We talk about the new guys—Sergey, Andy, and Aidyn—and I mention that I've never met Aidyn and don't even have an idea of what he looks like. That's incredibly unusual: before flying in space with someone, even someone from another country, you normally train with him or her, if only a little.

Kjell and I taste the lettuce we have been growing in space. August 2015.

Gennady offers to show me a picture. I decide it will be fun if I have no idea what he looks like until he comes floating through the hatch. Oleg and Gennady agree this will be entertaining.

It's a rare occasion for a Soyuz to dock without another one having left recently. The Soyuz that comes up today, September 24, is the one that will be my ride back to Earth six months from now. I'm looking forward to having some new faces up here, but I'm also concerned about how the Seedra will stand up to nine people exhaling CO_2 rather than six, as well as the strain on the toilets and other crucial equipment. The overall activity level is going to take some getting used to.

Our new crewmates will be Andreas Mogensen (Andy), Aidyn Aimbetov, and Sergey Volkov. Sergey will be here through the end of my mission and will command the Soyuz that he, Misha, and I will go home on in March, but Andy and Aidyn are here for only ten days.

Six weeks after Kjell, Kimiya, and Oleg's arrival, the new guys arrive, with Sergey Volkov floating through the hatch first. I know him well from being in the same era of space flyers—I was selected in NASA's 1996 class, and he was selected in Roscosmos's 1997 class, so we were peers. Sergey was Misha's backup for the yearlong mission, so when we were in Baikonur preparing for launch, Sergey was there with us, too.

Then Andy floats through the hatch. He's an ESA astronaut from Denmark whom I've known for years, a friendly guy, young in appearance with blond hair. He grew up all over the world and went to high school and college in the United States. His wife jokes that his English is better than his Danish.

When Aidyn comes floating through last, I'm watching with interest, and when I see him, I am surprised that I'm not surprised. He looked pretty much like what I thought a Kazakh cosmonaut and fighter pilot would look like—a Kazakh military man. He pauses in the hatch to give a heroic Superman pose to the camera, Gennady and Oleg holding his sides to steady him. The Russian space agency has been promising to send a Kazakh for a long time, to thank them for the use of Baikonur as the Russian launch operations center. Aidyn is the third Kazakh to go to space but the first to fly under his country's own flag rather than the Russian flag. He was assigned to the mission late, so he didn't get as extensive training as usual and there wasn't a detailed science program established for him to do.

From the start, Aidyn seems disoriented up here. He gets lost trying to find his way to the Soyuz and ends up in the U.S. lab module. The next day, he can't find the Japanese module. I find him looking for the 3-D printer in the U.S. segment, and we try to talk about it. But he speaks no English, and Russian is a second language for both of us, so our discussion is pretty basic.

Today we hold the change-of-command ceremony, so I am now officially the commander of the International Space Station. The capcom on the ground congratulates me on taking over for the next six months, and her words hit me—six months is a long time. I've been up here for so long, and I'm only halfway through.

In the morning, Gennady greets me, "Good morning, Comrade Commander," with great affection in his voice. I'm going to miss him next week when he's gone—he has been a great commander, and I have learned a lot from him.

Today is Friday, and because there are so many of us, we eat Friday dinner in Node 1 rather than trying to cram into the snug Russian service module. Andy has brought us some corned beef and cabbage, which hits the spot; I've been craving a corned beef sandwich from the Carnegie Deli in New York for a long time. After we're done eating, Andy hands each of us a Danish chocolate, an unexpected treat.

Our nine-person crew finds it hard to fit into one room for our Friday-night group dinner. Front row: Kimiya and Sergei; second row: Aidyn, Misha, Gennady, and me; third row: Andy and Kjell. Not pictured: Oleg. September 2015.

On Sunday, we have a traditional Kazakh meal, irradiated and packaged into space-food servings: horse meat soup, cheese made of horse milk, and horse milk to drink. The horse meat is a little gamey, but I eat all of it. The cheese is really salty, which is actually a nice change from the low-sodium food we generally have up here. As commander, I feel like I should try everything.

Unlike Aidyn, Andy is very busy. The European Space Agency has sent many science experiments with him. I feel bad for him, because he is spending most of his time on his own in the Columbus module, which is windowless. I check in with him often to see if he needs any help, and he always seems to be doing well. When Andy isn't working, he hangs out with us, watching TV or chatting. I encourage him to spend time looking out the window, but I get the sense he wants to be part of the crew just as much as he wants to enjoy the view.

While I like having new faces up here, we definitely feel the strain of having such a full house. With NASA's permission, Sergey sleeps in the U.S. airlock. Without asking permission from the Japanese space agency, I let Andy sleep in their module, since I want him to have some windows to enjoy the view. Aidyn sleeps in the habitation module of the Soyuz they will be going home on.

A few days later, I give myself a flu shot, the first one administered in space. We are safe from infectious illness up here, so the shot isn't to protect me. It's part of the Twins Study comparing Mark and me. He will inject himself with the same serum at the same time. Then our immunological responses will be compared.

I give myself a flu shot in space. Mark gives himself a flu shot on Earth. September 2015.

When we both tweet about our flu shots, the response is surprising. I even get retweeted by the Centers for Disease Control and the National Institutes of Health. Just the fact that I injected myself seems to be the subject of fascination. I'm learning that sometimes it's the small details of life in space that capture the public's attention the most.

On September 12, we gather to see off Gennady and the short-duration crew. Gennady has prepared their Soyuz and the crew is suited up in the underwear that go with their Sokol suits. We set up the cameras for the ground to watch as we gather in the service module, then make conversation as we wait awkwardly for the clock to tick down. When it's finally time for them to float through the hatch into the Soyuz, I hug each of them good-bye, especially Gennady. I tell him how much I'm going to miss him. When they are all in the Soyuz, I float in after them and joke that I'm going to stow away. "I'm done, guys, I've decided I'm going back with you!" Everyone laughs as I float back into the station.

We close the hatch, and a couple of hours later, they are gone.

20

FOR NEARLY AS long as human beings have been going into space, we have been determined to climb out of the spacecraft. It's partly just to achieve the fantasy of a human being floating alone in the immensity of the cosmos, nothing but an umbilical connecting him or her to the mother ship. But spacewalks are also a practical necessity for exploration. The ability to move from one spacecraft to another, to explore the surfaces of planets, or to perform maintenance, repairs, or assembly on the exterior of the spacecraft—all are crucial to long-term space travel.

The first spacewalk was carried out in 1965 by cosmonaut Alexei Arkhipovich Leonov. He opened the hatch of his Voskhod spacecraft, floated out on an umbilical, and reported to Moscow: "The Earth is absolutely round"—probably to the dismay of flat-earthers everywhere. It was a triumphant moment for the Soviet space program, but after twelve minutes, Alexei Arkhipovich found that he could not get back through the hatch. Due to a malfunction or poor design, his spacesuit had inflated so much that he could no longer fit through the narrow opening. He had to let some of the precious air out of his suit in order to struggle back through. Doing so caused the pressure to drop so much he nearly passed out. This was not an auspicious beginning to the history of spacewalks, but since then more than two hundred people have successfully suited up to float out an airlock into the blackness of space.

While some of the challenges of spacewalks have gotten easier, they are no less dangerous. Just a few years ago, astronaut Luca Parmitano's helmet began filling with water from his suit's cooling system while he was outside, and he almost drowned in space. Spacewalks are much riskier than any other part of our time in orbit—there are so many things that can go wrong. We are so vulnerable out there.

As pilot and commander of the space shuttle, I never had the chance to do a spacewalk. Shuttle pilots knew that we would never have the chance to put on a spacesuit and float out into the cosmos. A shuttle could return safely with a missing or injured mission specialist, but a missing pilot or commander would be much more problematic. We are now in a different era of spaceflight, and this mission on ISS has given me the chance.

It is October 28, and I have been up since five-thirty. I get into a diaper and the liquid cooling garment we wear under the spacesuits, like long underwear with built-in air-conditioning once it's connected to the suit. Then I eat a quick breakfast I'd laid out the night before to save time and make my way to the airlock to start getting suited up. My goal is to be out of the airlock early. My philosophy is that for complicated jobs, if you aren't ahead of schedule, you're already behind.

Kjell and I spend an hour breathing pure oxygen to reduce the amount of nitrogen in our blood so we won't get the bends (decompression sickness). Kimiya is the intravehicular crew member (IV) for this spacewalk, responsible for helping us get dressed, managing the procedure for prebreathing oxygen, and controlling the airlock and its systems. His job is critical for Kjell and me. It's practically impossible to get in and out of a spacesuit without help, and if Kimiya makes even the smallest mistake— puts on my boot incorrectly, for instance—I could die a horrible death. My suit includes a life support system that keeps oxygen flowing, scrubs the carbon dioxide that I exhale, and keeps cool water flowing through the tubes covering my body so I don't get overheated. Each suit costs about $12 million and weighs about 250 pounds on Earth. Although weightless, the suit still has mass. It's also stiff and bulky, making it difficult to maneuver. Once the suit is on and properly sealed, the last step is to put my helmet on. My visor has been fitted with corrective lenses so I won't have to wear glasses or contacts. Glasses can slip, especially when I'm working and sweating, and I can't adjust them when I'm wearing my helmet. Contact lenses would be an option, too, but they don't agree with my eyes.

Once we are suited up, Kimiya floats us into the airlock— first me, then Kjell—allowing us to save our energy for what is to come. We float and wait for the air to be pumped out of the airlock and back into the station. Air is a precious resource, so we don't like to vent it out into space.

"How you doing, Kjell?" I ask, staring directly at his boots.

"Great," Kjell says, and gives a quick thumbs-up I can barely see through the bottom of my visor. Suddenly a series of loud bangs reverberates through the airlock, a sound I've never heard in training. It's like someone knocking on a door loudly and urgently. Then it's quiet. Has something gone wrong? Should we be doing something? I mention the sound to the ground, and they tell me that it's normal, one of the things that happens when the air is sucked out of the airlock. No one thought to tell us about it in training, or maybe they just forgot to mention it, or maybe they did and I forgot. I've practiced this moment many times, wearing a spacesuit and being lowered into a giant swimming pool containing an ISS mock-up at the JSC, but it's different doing it for real, in space, with no safety divers to help us out if things go wrong.

Once the airlock is nearly at vacuum, Kjell and I do a series of checks on our spacesuits to make sure they are not leaking.

Looking ahead at the procedures, I see that once the airlock is down to a complete vacuum, each of us will turn our water switch on, which will allow water to flow through the cooling system to control the temperature in our suits. We can't do this too soon because in partial vacuum, liquid water can get into the wrong part of the suit and freeze and crack the lines. At full vacuum, the ice that cools the water in our suits sublimates—meaning it goes from a solid directly to a gas without going through the liquid phase. As the air continues to escape the airlock, I consider warning Kjell that the water switch is easy to flip accidentally. It's right next to a similar-looking switch that we use often to silence alarms or scroll through lines of status messages on a small LCD screen. But I tell myself that Kjell is as well trained as I am for this spacewalk. I'm not going to micromanage him.

When the airlock is not quite at a vacuum, Kjell says, "Houston—and Scott—I just hit my water switch on/off."

I take a breath to steady myself. "You cycled it?" I ask. He's just done the very thing I decided against warning him about.

"Yeah."

The only way to train for a spacewalk in zero gravity is in a deep pool. The spacesuit is so heavy in Earth's gravity that I need to be lifted into the pool by a machine. October 2013.

Our capcom for the spacewalk is Tracy Caldwell Dyson, my crewmate from my second shuttle flight—she gained a new last name through marriage since then. "Houston copies," Tracy responds. "Kjell, can you tell us how long it was on?"

"Less than half a second," Kjell says. He sounds dejected. We've already spent hours today—and entire working days over the past two weeks—getting ready for this spacewalk. We do not want to have to start all over, not to mention the possibility of damaging the expensive suit.

While spacesuit experts on Earth discuss how to proceed, I'm upset with myself for not warning Kjell. While we wait for NASA to decide if it's safe for Kjell to continue, I need to keep his head in the game.

"It's happened before, Kjell," I tell him. "It'll happen again."

"Yeah," Kjell answers, sounding miserable.

"Don't worry about it," I say, wishing the visor allowed me to make eye contact and see how he's doing.

"No worries," Kjell replies in a flat tone completely at odds with his words. Astronauts have seen their careers permanently affected by mistakes like this.

"It'll be all right," I say, talking to myself as much as I'm talking to him now.

Suit experts on the ground are still discussing whether to proceed. Meanwhile, we are told we can open the hatch and enjoy the view while they decide on a course of action. As I put my hand on the handle, I realize that I have no idea whether it will be day or night outside. I release the lock on the hatch handle that releases the "dogs." Now I have to simultaneously pull the hatch toward my chest and turn it toward my head, which is challenging, because with nothing to hook my feet onto, I'm pulling my-self toward the hatch almost as much as I'm pulling it toward me.

I tug and push and pull for a few minutes, and finally the hatch cracks open for my first view of space from outside the spacecraft. On Earth, we look at everything through the filter of the atmosphere, which dulls the light. But here, in the emptiness of space, the sun's light is white-hot and brilliant. The bright sun-shine bouncing off the Earth is overwhelmingly beautiful. I've just gone from grunting in annoyance at a piece of machinery to staring in awe at the most incredible view I've ever seen.

Inside my spacesuit, I feel like I'm in a tiny spacecraft rather than wearing something. My upper body floats inside the hard torso, my head encased in the helmet. I hear the comforting humming noise of the fan moving the air around inside my suit. The helmet has a faint chemical smell, not unpleasant, perhaps the anti-fog solution our visors are treated with. Through the ear-piece built into my comm cap, I can hear the voices of Tracy in Houston and Kjell just a few feet away from me out here in outer space—that, and the strangely amplified sound of my own breathing.

It takes the ground about ten minutes to tell us to go outside the hatch, where we can move around better, so I can check over Kjell's suit for a leak. In the cold of space, a leak would look like snow shooting out of the backpack of the suit. If I don't see snow-flakes, frozen water vapor escaping the suit, we may be allowed to continue.

I grab both handrails on either side of my head, getting ready to pull myself out. The airlock's hatch faces the Earth, which would seem to be in the direction we would call "down." In the training pool, the hatch was facing toward the floor, which always felt like down. Though I was neutrally buoyant in the pool, gravity still forced me toward the center of the Earth, providing a clear sense of up and down. For the hundreds of hours we practiced for this spacewalk, I got used to the idea of this configuration.

Once I'm about halfway through the hatch, though, I suddenly feel like I'm climbing up, as if out of the sunroof of a car. The large blue dome of Earth hovers over my head like some nearby alien planet in a sci-fi film, looking as if it could come crashing down upon us. For a moment, I'm disoriented. I'm thinking about where to look for the attachment point, a small ring where I will hook my safety tether, but I don't know where to look for it.

Like any highly trained pilot, I know how to compartmentalize, to push distracting thoughts out of my mind and focus on what is immediately in front of me—my gloves, the handrail, the small labels on the outside of the station I've familiarized myself with through countless hours of training. I must block out the looming Earth above and the feeling of disorientation it creates. I don't have time for it, so I set it aside and get to work. I secure my safety tether to one of the rings just outside the airlock, checking to make sure the hook is in fact closed and locked with complete certainty. Like putting an airplane's landing gear down before landing, this is one of those things you absolutely do not want to screw up.

During my last long-duration mission on ISS, two of the Russian cosmonauts, Oleg Skripochka and Fyodor Yurchikhin, did a spacewalk together to install some new equipment on the outside of the Russian service module. When the two of them came back inside, they both looked shaken, Oleg especially. I assumed at first his reaction was to being outside for the first time. It wasn't until my current mission that I learned that during their spacewalk, Oleg had become untethered from the station and started to float away. The only thing that saved him was hitting an antenna, sending him tumbling back toward the station close enough to grab on to a handrail, saving his life. I've often thought since about what we would have done if we'd known he was drifting irretrievably away from the station. It probably would have been possible to tie his family into the comm system in his spacesuit so they could say good-bye before the rising CO_2 or oxygen deprivation caused him to lose consciousness—not something I wanted to spend a lot of time thinking about during my own spacewalk.

The U.S. spacesuits include simple jet packs we could use to maneuver ourselves in space in case our tether breaks or we screw up. But we would not want to rely on this because the only practice we had using the jet packs was with virtual reality simulations. And some astronauts ended up running out of fuel or missing the space station altogether during the simulations. I'm very aware that if I become detached and run out of fuel, even if the station is just one inch from my glove tips, the result will be the same: I will die.

Once I'm certain my tether is secured, I remove Kjell's tether from me and attach it to the outside of the station as well, being just as careful to double-check it as I was with my own. Kjell starts handing me bags of equipment we will need for our work, and I secure each of them to the circular handrail outside the airlock. When we have everything we need, I give Kjell the go to exit. The first thing we do once we are both outside is our "buddy checks," looking over each other's suits from head to toe making sure everything is in order. Tracy talks us through it from mission control, telling me step-by-step how to check Kjell's PLSS (portable life support system, the "backpack" we wear with the spacesuit) for signs of damage. It looks completely normal—there are no snowflakes, I'm happy to report to the ground. Kjell and I both breathe a sigh of relief. Our spacewalk will proceed. Nearly five hours after getting into our spacesuits, we are ready to get to work.

Tracy's voice breaks the silence: "All right, guys, with Scott leading, we will begin translating out to your respective work sites."

By "translate," she means to move ourselves, hand over hand, along a path of rails attached to the outside of the station. On Earth, walking is done with the feet; in space, especially outside the station, it's done with the hands. This is one of the reasons why the gloves of our spacesuits are so critical.

"Roger that," I tell Tracy.

I move out to my first work site, on the right side of the giant truss of the space station, occasionally looking back to make sure my tether doesn't get snagged on anything. I'm immediately struck by how damaged the outside of the station is. Micrometeoroids and orbital debris have been striking it for fifteen years, creating small pits and scrapes as well as holes that completely penetrate the handrails, creating jagged edges. It's a little alarming—especially when I'm out here with nothing but a few layers of spacesuit between me and the next strike.

Being outside is clearly an unnatural act. I'm not scared, which I guess is a testament to our training and to my ability to compartmentalize. If I were to take a moment to think about what I'm doing, I might completely freak out. When the sun is up, I can feel its intense heat. When it sets, forty-five minutes later, I can feel the depths of the cold, from plus to minus 270 degrees Fahrenheit in minutes. We have glove heaters to keep our fingers from freezing but nothing for our toes. My feet quickly become so cold it's distracting. (When I come back inside and get out of the suit, I will find that my feet are blue.)

The color and brilliance of Earth, sprawling out in every direction, are startling. I've seen the planet from spacecraft windows countless times now, but the difference between seeing it from inside a spacecraft, through multiple layers of bulletproof glass, and seeing it from out here is like the difference between seeing a mountain from a car window and climbing the peak. My clear plastic visor allows me to see in every direction. I take in the stunning blue, the texture of the clouds, the varied landscapes of the planet, the glowing atmosphere edging on the horizon, a delicate sliver that makes all life on Earth possible. There is nothing but the black vacuum of the cosmos beyond. I want to say something about it to Kjell, but nothing I can think of sounds right.

My first task is to remove insulation from a main bus switching unit—a giant circuit breaker that moves power from the solar arrays to the ISS equipment—so the unit can later be removed by the main robotic arm.

Kjell's first task is to put a thermal blanket on the Alpha Magnetic Spectrometer (AMS), a particle physics experiment. It's been sending back the kind of data that could change our understanding of the universe, but it needs to be protected from the sun if it's going to continue doing its job—it's getting too hot. The AMS was delivered to the station by the last flight of *Endeavour* in 2011, which was commanded by my brother. Neither of us would have guessed five years ago that I would be leading a spacewalk to extend its lifespan.

Instruments like the AMS and the Hubble Space Telescope have transformed our understanding of the universe in recent years. For example, Hubble's observations have shown that there are in fact ten times as many galaxies as we had previously thought—2 trillion instead of 200 billion.

The focus required to do even simple work in the zero g of space is daunting, similar to the focus required to land an F-14 Tomcat on an aircraft carrier, or land the space shuttle. But in this case, I have to maintain that focus all day, rather than for only a matter of minutes.

When I finish removing the insulation from the main bus unit and stuffing it into a bag, I get congratulations from the ground for a job well done. For the first time in hours, I take a deep breath, stretch as best I can in the stiff spacesuit, and look around. This would normally be a good time to break for lunch, but that's not on today's schedule. I can sip water through a straw in my helmet, but that's it. I'm making good time and still have a lot of energy. *We are going to be able to nail this spacewalk,* I think. As the day goes on, it will become clear that this is a false sense of confidence.

The next task for me is working on the end effector, the "hand" of the robot arm. Without it, we can't capture and bring in the visiting vehicles that deliver food and other necessities to the U.S. side of the station (that is, of course, when they don't crash or explode first).

While I was training for this mission, I practiced greasing a replica of this end effector, using tools identical to the ones I'm using up here. While I practiced, I wore a duplicate of my spacesuit gloves.

But the experience is still disorientingly different now that I, the grease gun, and the grease are all floating in space, with the sun rising and setting spectacularly every ninety minutes, and the planet spinning majestically underfoot. For several hours, I use this tool like a five-year-old with finger paint. The grease goes everywhere. Small beads of grease jump off the gun as if they have a will of their own to explore the cosmos. Some of them come right toward me, which could pose a serious problem. If grease starts to coat the faceplate of my helmet, I may not be able to see to find my way back in. This task is taking much longer than had been scheduled, and soon my hands are aching to the point where I start to think I might not be able to move them. I work with Kimiya as he moves the robot arm to exactly where I need it. I put grease on the end of a long wire tool and stick it into the dark hole of the robot hand. I can't see in there and can only hope the grease is going in the right place.

This task is taking so long I know I won't get to complete some of our other scheduled activities. Kjell is running long, too. We are well past the six-and-a-half-hour mark when we start getting organized to call it a day and head back to the airlock. We still have the toughest part of the spacewalk in front of us—getting ourselves back into the airlock. Kjell goes first and guides his bulky suit through the opening without getting caught on anything. Once inside, he attaches his waist tether. Next I release his safety tether, which is still connected to the outside of the station, and attach it to myself, then release my own. I swing my legs over my head and flip upside down into the airlock so I will be facing the hatch to close it.

Closing the hatch, absolutely mandatory, will be much harder than opening it, with the fatigue from the spacewalk taking its toll. My hands are completely shot.

Although I have been an astronaut for decades, this was my first time walking and working in space. On our first spacewalk, Kjell and I installed some insulating blankets on the Alpha Magnetic Spectrometer and repaired the station's robotic arm. November 6, 2015.

The first step is to close the thermal cover of the hatch, which has been severely damaged by the sun, like most of the equipment exposed to its harsh rays. The cover doesn't fit right anymore—it's now the shape of a potato chip—and it takes a lot of tries to get it secured properly. But it is important because in its proper position, it becomes a blanket covering the hatch on the outside of the space station. With the thermal cover closed, it's time to get hooked back up to the umbilical that provides oxygen, water, and power to the suits from the station's systems rather than using the suit's self-contained system. This isn't an easy task either, but after a few minutes, we manage to get them connected properly.

Even though I'm exhausted, I manage to get the hatch securely closed and locked. As the air hisses in around us, Kjell and I are breathing hard from the work of getting back inside. We will have a wait of about fifteen minutes to make sure the hatch is properly closed while the airlock returns to the pressure of the station.

We have been in these suits for eleven hours now.

We both know we will have to do another spacewalk in nine days.

When the hatch opens and we see Kimiya's smiling face, we know we are nearly done. Kimiya and Oleg do a close inspection of our gloves and take many pictures of them to send to the ground. Any holes will be easier to see while our suits are still pressurized.

When we are finally ready to get out of the suits, Kimiya helps us remove our helmets first, which is a relief in one way. But we will miss the cleaner air: the CO_2 scrubbers in the suits do a much better job than Seedra. My suit and I are floating together, so I need Kimiya to hold on to the arms of the suit and pull hard while he pushes down on the pants in the other direction with his legs.

Once I'm out of the spacesuit, it hits me all at once how draining it's been just being in the suit, never mind the full day of grueling work I did while wearing it. Kjell and I head to the PMM, where we remove our long underwear and dispose of our used diapers and biomedical sensors. We take a quick "shower" (move the dried sweat around on our bodies with wipes, then towel off to dry) and eat some food for the first time in fourteen hours.

A few days later, I stop Kjell when he is floating through the U.S. lab and ask him if he could spare a minute. I put on a serious face and tell him I need to talk with him.

"Sure, what's up?" Kjell responds with his characteristic upbeat tone.

"It's about the next spacewalk," I say with a serious tone. I pause as if I'm searching for the right words.

"Yeah?" Kjell says, now with a hint of apprehension.

"I'm afraid I have to tell you—you're not going to be EV Two." EV2 was the role Kjell had played on our first spacewalk—I was the leader (EV1) as the more experienced astronaut, though it was the first time outside for both of us.

A look of concern crosses Kjell's face, followed quickly by sincere disappointment. He thinks he's been removed from the next spacewalk altogether.

"Okay," he answers, waiting to hear more.

I decide I've messed with him enough. "Kjell, you're going to be EV One."

It was a mean trick, but it's worth it to see the relief and excitement on his face when he realizes that he has been promoted. Kjell will fly more future missions and likely will conduct more future spacewalks, so it will be invaluable for him to get experience as the leader. I have full confidence in his ability to carry out this role, and I tell him so. We have a lot of preparation to do.

November 3 is a midterm election day on Earth, so I call the voting commission in my home county—Harris County, Texas—and get a password that I can use to open a PDF they emailed to me earlier; I fill out my ballot and email it back to them. I take pride in exercising my constitutional rights from space, and I hope it sends a message that voting is important (and that inconvenience is never a good excuse for failing to vote).

21

NOVEMBER BRINGS WITH it the need to prepare for our second spacewalk. It also marks the nine-year anniversary of my surgery, and I realize that I have spent more than a year of my life in space *after* having been diagnosed with and treated for cancer. I hope my story is helpful to others facing cancer or other serious illnesses, to show that you can still achieve great things after being seriously ill.

Once again, Kjell and I have spent days preparing. This spacewalk will have two goals: one is to work on a cooling system. The other is to fill that cooling system's ammonia supply. These tasks might sound unexciting, but we need to do this to keep the space station cool despite getting roasted by the unfiltered sun for forty-five minutes out of every ninety.

November 6, the day of our second spacewalk, starts much like our first: up early, quick breakfast, prebreathe oxygen, get suited up. Today I've decided to wear my glasses, because I found the corrective lenses built into my visor didn't work as well as I'd hoped last time. There are risks involved in wearing my glasses—if they slip off, there will be nothing I can do about it with my helmet on, but I prepare for that problem by taping them to my head. Being bald, I have the perfect haircut for this technique.

Our work site today will be all the way out at the end of the truss, 150 feet from the airlock—so far that we need to use the length of both our safety tethers together to reach it. As we start the journey, moving hand over hand along the rails, I notice again how much damage has been done to the outside of the station by micrometeoroids and orbital debris. It's remarkable to see the pits in the metal handrails going all the way through like bullet holes. I'm shocked again to see them.

Our ground IV today is a veteran astronaut I've known for fifteen years, Megan McArthur. Despite being one of the youngest astronauts when she was selected, at twenty-eight, she's always been calm and sure of herself, even under pressure. With her help, Kjell and I get ourselves and our tools out to the work site, ready to go.

Our first task is a two-person job: removing a cover from a metal box and opening a valve to allow the flow of ammonia.

Kjell Lindgren and I work together to restore the port truss ammonia cooling system to its original configuration during our second spacewalk, which lasted seven hours and forty-eight minutes. November 6, 2015.

Kjell and I easily get into a rhythm where it seems as though we can read each other's minds, and it feels as if Megan is right there in lockstep with us. We work together with an uncanny level of efficiency. Even though I'm not superstitious, I don't want to jinx things by saying, "This is going great" or "This is turning out to be pretty easy." We just need to keep it up until we are done.

When we get the cover back on the box, Kjell and I separate to work on different tasks for a while. He continues working on the ammonia lines, and I work on the vent lines on the back side of the space station's truss. Both are difficult tasks, and they take our full attention. The space station uses high-concentration ammonia to cool the electronics—not the ammonia you might have found under your grandmother's sink, but something a hundred times stronger and much more lethal. If this ammonia were to get inside the station, we could all be dead within minutes. We must make sure not to get any of the ammonia onto our suits.

As I had learned on my first spacewalk, every time I adjust my tethers, move a tool on my mini-workstation, or even just move, I have to concentrate with every bit of my attention, making sure I'm doing the right thing at the right time in the right way. I must double-check that I'm not getting tangled up in my safety tether, floating away from the structure, or losing my tools.

After a few hours, I head back toward the CETA cart (CETA stands for Crew and Equipment Translation Aid), which is like one of those manual handcars once used on railways. It travels along a track with the mobile transporter, and together they allow us to move heavy equipment and tools and can carry the robotic arm used to capture supply ships. I have been tasked with tying down the brake handle on the CETA so no one can accidentally lock the brake. I worried that this task took me too far away from Kjell if he needed help, but the lead flight director thought I could do both tasks.

I am working mostly on my own, using reminders written on a checklist on my wrist, as Megan is talking Kjell through his much more complex task. As I continue working, I can hear Kjell struggling with the ammonia connections. These can require all your strength, even for a strong guy like him. And he needs to take more than twenty steps for each connection, all while remaining alert in case ammonia shoots out and contaminates his suit.

I finish up and take one last look over my work site, making sure everything looks right, before heading back out to the end of the truss to help Kjell. Hand over hand, it takes me a few minutes to get to him. We're preparing to vent the ammonia system—Kjell opens a valve and quickly moves clear. High-pressure ammonia streams out the back of the space station like a giant cloud of snow. As we watch, the sun catches the huge plume, its particles glistening against the blackness of space. It's a moment of unexpected beauty, and we float there for a minute, taking it in.

When the venting seems to be complete, Megan instructs us to separate—Kjell will stay here and work on cleaning up the ammonia vent tool while I head back to the solar array joint to put a tool away, a complicated hose called a jumper. Megan talks me through the process. I struggle with one of the connections, the end of the hose with a valve.

I work with it for a few more minutes before getting it configured the way it's supposed to be.

"Okay," I report. "Forward white band visible."

"Okay, Scott, I copy the forward white band is visible—check the detent button is up."

"It's up."

When I hear Megan's voice again, there is a subtly different tone.

"I'm going to ask you to pause right here, and I'm going to tell you guys what we've got going on."

She doesn't say what this pause is about, but Kjell and I know: Megan has just been given some news within mission control, something the flight directors have to make a quick decision about. It may be something that puts us in danger. She doesn't leave us hanging for long.

"Okay. Currently, guys, from a momentum management perspective, we're getting close to a Loss of Attitude Control (LOAC) condition," she says. She means the gyroscopes that control the station's position in the sky have become saturated by the venting ammonia. Soon we will lose control of our position, and when that happens, we will soon lose communication with the ground. This is a dangerous situation, just as we anticipated.

Megan continues. "So what we need Kjell to do is to pull out of your current activity and head over toward the radiator. We're going to have you redeploy it."

If we can't put away this radiator properly, we will have to put it back out in its extended position.

"Copy," Kjell answers crisply.

"You've probably gathered from a timeline perspective where we're going," Megan says. "We're going to have you clean up the vent tool eventually, Kjell. And, Scott, you're going to continue

with the jumper, but we are not going after cinching and shroud-
ing the radiator today. It will take too long."

We both acknowledge her. This situation with the gyroscopes
is serious enough to change our plans. Even under the best of
circumstances, when we hear we are close to saturating the gyros,
it's one of those "Oh no" moments. The station won't start spinning out of control like a carnival ride, but losing communication
with Megan and all the experts on the ground is never a good
thing. And with the two of us outside, a communication blackout
would add a new danger to an already risky situation.

If we can't talk to the ground, we lose the expertise of the
thousands of people in Houston, Moscow, and other sites all over
the world who understand every aspect of the systems keeping us
alive up here. Our spacesuits, the life support systems within the
station, the Soyuz meant to get us back safely to Earth, the science experiments that are the reason for us being here in the first
place—our comm system is our only connection to the experts on
all of these. Our only connection to Earth. We have no choice but
to take the risk.

I think about just how alone Kjell and I are out here. The
ground wants to help us, but we may not be able to hear them.
Our crewmates inside the station would do anything to ensure
our safety, but they may not be able to reach us. Kjell and I have
to count on each other. Our lives are in our own hands.

As instructed, we re-extend the spare radiator rather than taking the time to cinch it down and install a thermal cover. It will
be safe like this until a future spacewalk can finish the job. We are
nearing the seven-hour mark, the point where we were planning
to head back to the airlock, but we are still far away with much left

to do before we can get inside. We start the process of cleaning up our work site and checking our tool bags and mini-workstations to make sure we aren't leaving anything behind. Once everything is packed up and checked, we start the hard process of traveling hand over hand back to where we started.

We are about halfway to the airlock when I hear Megan's voice again in my headset.

"Scott, if you're okay with it, we need you to go back to the vent valves and make sure they are in the right configuration. The specialists are seeing some data they aren't happy with."

This is a simple request, but Megan's tone communicates a lot—she wants me to know this action is not required and that I can say no without causing any problems. It's a task that could easily be left for the next astronauts, who will be launching next month. She knows that we have been outside a long time and are exhausted. My body is aching, my feet are cold, my knuckles are rubbed raw. I've been sweating and am dehydrated. There is still so much we have to do before we can get safely back inside, es- pecially if anything unexpected happens between now and then.

I answer her right away, putting a vigor into my voice that I don't actually feel. "Sure, no problem," I say.

I've been convincing myself all day that I actually feel fine, that I have plenty of energy left. Both Kjell's life and my own de- pend on our ability to push past our limits. I've convinced myself so effectively that I've convinced the ground team, too.

I head to the back side of the truss again to check the vent valves. It's dark now and starting to get cold. I don't waste the effort to adjust the cooling on my suit—even just that simple ges- ture would hurt my hands too much. I would rather just freeze.

But in the darkness, I get turned around and upside down. I can see only what's immediately in front of my face, like a scuba diver in murky waters, and it's completely disorienting. Everything looks unfamiliar in the dark. (One difference between the Russian approach to spacewalking and ours is that the Russians stop working when it's dark; the cosmonauts just hang on to the side of the station and rest, waiting for the sun to come up again. This is safer in one sense—they are probably less likely to make mistakes, and to tire—but they also have to do twice as many spacewalks because they work only half the time they are outside.)

I start to head in a direction I think is the right one, then realize it's wrong, but I can't tell whether I'm upside down or right side up. I read some mile markers—numbers attached to the handrails—to Megan, hoping she can help tell me where I am.

"It looks much different in the dark," I tell Megan.

"Roger that," she says.

"Did I not go far enough?" I ask. "Let me go back to my safety tether." I figure once I find the place where my tether is attached I'll be able to get my bearings.

"We're working on cuing up the sun for you," Megan jokes, "but it's going to be another five minutes."

I look in the direction I think is Earth, hoping to catch a glimpse of some city lights 250 miles below in the darkness to get my bearings. If I just knew which way Earth is, I could figure out where I am on the truss. When I look around, all I see is black. Maybe I'm looking right at the Earth and not seeing any lights because we're passing over the Pacific Ocean, or perhaps I'm just looking at space.

"Scott, can you see the PMM?"

I can't, but I don't want to give up. I see a tether that I think is Kjell's—if it is, I might be able to figure out where I am.

"Scott," Megan says, "we're just going to send you back now—we don't need to get this, so just head back to where your tether location is and then head back to the airlock." She takes an upbeat tone, as if this is good news, but she knows it will be frustrating to me to hear they're giving up on me.

As I search for my tether, I catch a glimpse of lights above me. I'm not sure what it is at first, since above me is what I thought was the blackness of space. But as the lights come into focus, I see they are city lights—the unmistakable lights of the Middle East, Dubai, and Abu Dhabi, stretched along the Persian Gulf standing out against the blackness of the water and the desert sands.

The lights reorient me—what I'd thought was down is up— and I feel the strange sensation of my internal gyroscope righting itself. Suddenly it's clear where I am and where I need to go.

"I see the PMM now, so I think I'm close," I tell her. "I can go do it. I'd prefer to do it if you guys are okay with it."

A pause. I know Megan is consulting with the flight director about whether to let me continue or tell me to come back inside.

"Okay, Scott, we're going to take your lead. We're happy to have you go and do that."

"Okay. I think I'm in good shape now."

When I reach the work site, the sun finally shines over the horizon while Megan talks me through the steps of configuring the vent valve on the ammonia tank. Once I'm done, Megan tells us to head back to the airlock.

I think about making a joke to the ground by calling myself "Magellan," in reference to the first explorer to circumnavigate the globe—a nickname we used to use in the Navy for those who get lost. But they might not get it, and besides, Magellan was killed before he made it home. I don't want to jinx myself.

I head back to the airlock, where I climb in first this time and get my tether secured so Kjell can follow. He crams himself in behind me. As he struggles to close the hatch, I try to hook up the oxygen and cooling line to my suit. But my hands are so tired I'm fumbling. To make things worse, my glasses moved and I can't see the connection. I struggle for a good ten minutes, by which time Kjell has moved himself into a position where he can see my connection and help me out. Working together, we get it connected. This is why we do spacewalks in pairs.

Kjell gets the hatch closed, and the air hisses in around us. The carbon dioxide in Kjell's suit is showing an elevated reading, so when the airlock finishes repressurizing, Kimiya and Sergey hurry to get him out of his helmet first. Through my visor, I can see that he is okay, nodding and talking. It will be ten minutes before Kimiya can take my helmet off for me. Kjell and I are attached to opposite walls, facing each other, held in place by the racks that secure our spacesuits. We have been in these suits for almost eleven hours. While I float there and wait to get out of my helmet, Kjell and I don't have to talk—we just share a look, the same look you'd give someone if you'd been riding down a familiar street together, chatting about this and that, and missed by nanoseconds being killed by an oncoming train. It's the look that says we both know we were at the limit of our abilities and it could have killed us.

Hours later, Kjell and I pass in the U.S. lab. "There ain't going to be no rematch," I say, quoting from the movie *Rocky*.

"I don't want one," says Kjell, laughing.

We have no way of knowing it yet, but only one of us is done with spacewalks.

Carrying my tool bags during the spacewalk. The solar panel behind me looks like a giant guitar. November 6, 2015.

22

ON DECEMBER 6, a Cygnus resupply launches successfully from Cape Canaveral. The module is named *Deke Slayton II* after one of the Mercury astronauts (the first Deke Slayton Cygnus blew up on launch the previous year). In addition to the regular supplies of food, clothes, oxygen, and other stuff, Cygnus is also carrying experiments and supplies to support research in biology, physics, medicine, and Earth science. It's also carrying a microsatellite deployer and the first microsatellite to be deployed from ISS. And, important to only me, on board is a gorilla suit sent by my brother to replace the one lost on Dragon. Once Cygnus safely reaches orbit—a stage we no longer take for granted after all the disasters earlier this year—Kjell captures it with the robot arm, his first time doing so.

A few days later, on December 11, we gather to say good-bye to Kjell, Kimiya, and Oleg. I remember when they arrived here about five months ago, which seems like another lifetime. Kjell and Kimiya, who showed up like helpless baby birds, are leaving as soaring eagles. They are now seasoned space flyers who can move around the station with ease, fix hardware of all kinds, run science experiments across multiple disciplines, and generally handle anything that comes their way without my help. I'm the only astronaut to witness the beginning and the end of someone else's long-duration spaceflight. I've known at some level how much astronauts learn and improve over the course of a single long-duration mission, but it's another thing entirely to witness it. I say good-bye knowing I still have three months ahead of me. I'll miss them.

Kjell prepares to capture a Cygnus cargo vehicle using Canadarm 2. December 4, 2015.

Yuri Malenchenko, Tim Kopra, and Tim Peake launch from Baikonur on December 15 at eleven a.m. our time and dock after a six-and-a-half-hour trip. I watch from the Cupola as they approach us, the black-and-white Soyuz with its solar panels spread like an insect's wings, a sight I never quite get used to. The capsule starts out so tiny it looks like a toy, like a scale model of itself, at times appearing to be on fire as the sunlight reflects off its surface. But then it gets bigger and bigger, slowly revealing itself to be a full-size spacecraft.

After a leak check, which takes a couple of hours this time—we open the hatch and welcome our three new crewmates aboard. As always, their first day is a full one. Throughout, I'm aware that this is the last time I will introduce new people to space, and it gives me a strangely sad feeling, a kind of pre-nostalgia.

I don't know Yuri especially well, though he is one of the most experienced space travelers in history. He has a reputation for being technically brilliant and has flown in space five times, including a long-duration mission on *Mir*, a space shuttle mission, and three previous long-duration missions on the International Space Station for a total of 641 days in space. He also has the distinction of being the only person to have gotten married while in space—on his first ISS mission, in 2003, he and his bride, Ekaterina, exchanged vows via videoconference while her friends and family gathered around her at home in Houston. (They're still married!)

Tim Kopra was an Army aviator and engineer before joining NASA in the 2000 class. He went to West Point and is a colonel in the Army. He also has multiple master's degrees and has been an astronaut for fifteen years, but this is only his second time in space.

Tim Peake was a helicopter test pilot in the United Kingdom until he became the first Brit chosen by the European Space Agency. This is his maiden voyage to space, making him the only rookie on the crew. For the UK, Tim is sort of their Yuri Gagarin and Alan Shepard rolled into one. That's a lot to live up to, but as our mission together goes on, I will come to find that he is more than up to it.

As always with newcomers to the space station, Tim and Tim

are as awkward and clumsy as toddlers. Sometimes when I want to help one of them get to where he needs to be, or want to get one of them out of the way quickly, I find it's easiest to physically grab him by the shoulders or the hips and move him around in space the way I'd move a bulky piece of cargo. Neither of them seems to mind.

The next day, I hear during the daily planning conference that we have a problem. The mobile transporter—the same one I worked on during my second spacewalk with Kjell—is stuck. Flight controllers had tried to move it so the robotic arm would be in position to work on it. But it quickly became stuck in an unsafe position, which would make dockings impossible for future visiting vehicles. The moment I hear these words, my heart sinks. I immediately know what went wrong: when I was working on the CETA cart, I must have accidentally locked the brake handles.

"I think I know who screwed this up," I tell Houston.

Later, I get on the phone with the flight director and tell her I'm almost certain about the brake handle.

There is a pause on the other end of the connection. "How certain are you?" she asks.

"Very certain," I say. I know what my answer will mean: I will have to do an unplanned spacewalk before the Progress can dock, and it's launching a week from tomorrow, so we'll have a terrifyingly short period of time to prepare, both in space and on Earth.

It's important to me to admit mistakes immediately, and I don't make excuses. If some other piece of equipment had been left in the wrong position, we could likely wait until the next scheduled spacewalk, even if it was months away, to fix it. But in addition to preventing visiting vehicles from docking, the stuck cart prevents us from moving the station in order to avoid debris or to use the robot arm for anything else. I start mentally preparing myself to go outside for the third time. I share the news with the crew, and they say they will help in any way necessary. The next day, NASA makes the official decision that we will try to fix the transporter on an emergency spacewalk.

It's hard enough to prepare for a spacewalk under ideal circumstances; it's much harder to do it on short notice and with colleagues who are still getting used to this strange environment. Tim Kopra, though an experienced astronaut, has been here only a few days and is still adjusting to living in space. He will have to get into a spacesuit and go outside with me. Tim Peake, who is still figuring out the most basic aspects of life up here, like eating and sleeping, will have to serve as IV. Both of them will have little margin for error in their demanding jobs.

Meanwhile, the Russians spend the next few days packing trash into the Progress that will be departing soon to burn up in the atmosphere. They have some extra room and ask if we want to put trash on board. Like many things in space—oxygen, water, food—trash removal capacity is a resource, and our two countries trade it like currency. I give them a couple of our large trash bags without telling Houston. I've been sneaking trash off the space station when the Russians have room for it all year, and we do the same for them, too, when we can. (This will cause a problem later when we pack the Cygnus and don't have all the trash Houston thinks we should—ten bags. After a lot of questions, I eventually tell them, "The trash fairy must have come in the middle of the night." No one mentions it again, which is a relief.) On December 19, I watch from the Russian service module as this Progress leaves. Now that it's gone, we have room for the new Progress that will launch in a few days. I realize the next time something pushes away from the station, two and a half months from now, I will be on it.

The next morning, I find an email from the ground asking me to submit a guest list for my landing. A limited number of people will be allowed to come to mission control in Houston to watch on the big screens as our Soyuz lands in Kazakhstan. I picture the spectator area in mission control, my friends and family gathered there and watching as our capsule falls through the atmosphere and lands—we hope—safely on the desert steppes of Kazakhstan.

Suddenly it occurs to me that making this list is the first thing I am doing to prepare for my return to Earth. From now on, I will do more and more—throwing things out, packing things up, making more lists, thinking about what my next steps will be in life. I have a lot more time in space to go, but as of today, a small part of my mind is on my future on Earth.

On Monday, December 21, I wake up early, diaper up, and get into my liquid cooling garment for the third time. Tim Kopra and I start our prebreathe of pure oxygen; then an hour later Tim Peake helps us get into our spacesuits. This spacewalk will be shorter than the previous ones. We will get the CETA cart and the mobile transporter, then use them to do a couple more tasks we know will need to be done at some point (called get-ahead tasks) so as to make the best use of the time and resources it takes just to get suited up and get out the door. Tim Peake does a great job as IV—as he moves through the checklist to get us ready (with the help of Sergey Volkov), any concern I might have had about whether he was prepared to take on this role after being up here for only six days dissolves. He works efficiently and confidently, and soon we are in the airlock and doing our leak checks.

I'm EV1 again. I feel more confident on my third spacewalk. When the airlock is fully depressurized, Tim Kopra and I switch our suits to battery power and the spacewalk has officially begun. This is Tim's second spacewalk, but his first was in 2009, so it's been a while. Once we are outside and have completed our buddy checks, I move hand over hand to the mobile transporter. When I reach the cart, I try moving it along the truss, and sure enough, it's stuck. I release the locked brake handle, then move it freely in both directions. The ground is satisfied.

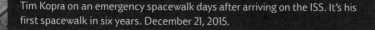

Tim Kopra on an emergency spacewalk days after arriving on the ISS. It's his first spacewalk in six years. December 21, 2015.

It feels odd to have accomplished our main objective only forty-five minutes in. We finish up some of the tasks that Kjell and I had to leave undone the last time we were out here and come back inside after three hours and fifteen minutes. While I'm far from the exhaustion I felt at the end of my earlier spacewalks, I'm still tired and sore.

After I come back in, I speak with Amiko and then check my email. There is one from Kjell, telling me he had watched the spacewalk. It's strange to imagine him in Houston, watching in the predawn early morning, sitting in a chair of some kind, gravity holding him there. "You guys crushed it!" his email reads.

Today is Christmas Eve, my third in space. This isn't a record anyone would envy, especially a parent with kids. A holiday that celebrates family togetherness can be the toughest time to be away. On top of that, I have worked nearly two weeks without a day off, so my mood going into Christmas is less than festive.

Holiday or not, today is just another workday on the schedule, one that becomes more difficult when the weight-lifting machine breaks down. This is more of an emergency than it might seem, because exercise is nearly as important to our well-being as oxygen and food. When we skip even one exercise session, we can feel it physically, as if our muscles are atrophying, and it's not a good feeling. Tim Kopra and I take nearly half the day to fix the machine. Because of this, we don't wrap up our workday until eight p.m. Then I make my way to the Russian segment for dinner. The Russians don't celebrate Christmas at the same time we do—the Orthodox calendar has Christmas on January 7—but they are happy to host a festive meal for the rest of us. I discover that the nutritionists in charge of our food have not bothered to create a special holiday meal, so I eat turkey cold cuts doused in a salty brine as Christmas Eve dinner. We do, however, have some hard salami that came up on Cygnus and some of that black, tarry caviar from the Russians, as well as some fresh onions and apples that came up on Progress yesterday, which we enjoy. We listen to Christmas music and the new Coldplay album I recently uplinked, which everyone likes. Our little celebration has chased away my bad mood. We toast our privileged spot in space, how lucky we are to be here and how much it means to us. We toast our family and friends back on Earth. We toast one another, our crewmates, the only six people off the planet for Christmas.

An hour and a half later, I get my scheduled videoconference with my kids. Samantha has traveled from Houston to Virginia Beach to be with her mother and sister for the holiday, and I'm pleased to see my girls together.

A videoconference with my daughters, Charlotte and Samantha, is the best part of my holiday in space. December 25, 2015.

I don't get much sleep, and in the morning, I float awake in my sleeping bag, putting off starting my day. Christmas mornings when I was growing up in New Jersey, my brother and I used to leap up even before it was fully light and run to the living room in our underwear to find our presents. When they were little, my daughters did the same. Later, I will spend this Christmas doing some public affairs events, where I know I will be asked what it's like to spend Christmas in space. I plan to say that being here at this special time gives me a chance to reflect on the holiday and how lucky we are to be able to see this view of our planet. But I will also say how much I miss being with the people I love.

That night, I read a few pages of the Shackleton book in my sleeping bag. On Christmas 1914, the first officer of the expedition wrote in his journal, "Here endeth another Christmas Day. I wonder how and under what circumstances our next one will be spent. Temperature 30 degrees." He couldn't have imagined how he would spend his next Christmas—camping on an ice floe with minimal provisions after their ship, the *Endurance*, had been crushed by ice. For all the suffering of their ordeal, the men found they enjoyed the self-reliance they had found. "In some ways they had come to know themselves better," Lansing writes. "In this lonely world of ice and emptiness, they had achieved at least a limited kind of contentment. They had been tested and found not wanting."

I, too, have been tested and found not wanting this Christmas. I turn out the light and float for a while before falling asleep.

New Year's Eve is a bigger holiday than Christmas on the space station because it's celebrated by every nation on the same day. We gather in the Russian segment for the festivities. We all have something to eat, someone makes a toast. We enjoy each other's company into the night. We briefly turn out the lights to see whether we can glimpse any fireworks on Earth—on my previous long-duration flight we were able to see the tiny specks of colored light, but this year we don't see any. It is still great to be spending my second New Year's Eve in space, and I'm glad I'm still able to appreciate the privilege of where I am and what I am getting to do. The next morning I wake up early to call my friends and family in the United States to wish them a happy 2016—the year I will come home.

23

TOMORROW, JANUARY 8, is the fifth anniversary of the shooting in Tucson that injured my sister-in-law, Gabby. I think about how far she has come, and how much she has lost. Five years ago, I was orbiting 250 miles above my family when they needed me most. So much has changed since then, yet I'm in the same place, doing the same thing, as we honor the victims of the shooting with a moment of silence.

A week later, the Seedra in Node 3 fails again. I've been daring to hope that I could get back to Earth without having to mess with the beast again, but no such luck.

The next day, Tim Kopra and I slide the beast out of its rack, move it to Node 2, secure it to a work bench, and take it apart. When I took this machine apart with Terry Virts, it was a multi-day operation that left him bandaged and both of us tired and frustrated. Today, the repair is going much better than it had previously. I've had so much experience with this machine that I can work on it with an incredible level of confidence and efficiency. At this point, I could write a repair manual for this thing if I wanted to. I can't help taking some pride in that. I also hope I will never have to take it apart again.

Later in the day, I'm working in the Japanese module when I

come across a drink bag, an aluminum pouch with a straw that we use instead of cups, wedged behind a piece of equipment. I pull it out and find it's marked with the initials DP. No one up here has the initials DP, or has in a long time. It must have belonged to Don Pettit, who was last here in 2012. I save the bag until Don is working as capcom, then hold it up in front of the camera and ask, "Is this your drink bag?"

Don laughs at the absurdity of the situation. At home you would never put down a glass of water and lose it for three years, but up here, it's incredibly easy to lose your drink or anything else.

A few days later, I take a great picture of the city of Houston and the Gulf Coast on a beautiful night pass. When I send it to Amiko, I use the word "home," and I'm surprised to find that I'm starting to set my internal compass there again. I'm starting to allow myself to look forward to getting back.

Later in January, we see through the second major botanical project on board the station. Growing lettuce back in August was relatively easy—we set up nutrient "pillows" under the grow light in the European module, watered the plants according to schedule, and watched the leaves sprout as expected for an easy harvest. Now I am growing flowering plants, zinnias, which we expect to be more difficult because the plants are more delicate and less forgiving. The sequence was set up this way on purpose—we will use what we learned from growing an easier, less demanding species to aid us in growing something more finicky.

The zinnias prove to be even more difficult than we expected. They often look unhealthy, and I suspect that our communication lag between space and the ground is to blame. I take pictures of the plants and send them to scientists on Earth, who, after looking them over and consulting among themselves, send me instructions about what to do—usually "water them" or "don't water them." By the time I get the instructions, things have gone too far in one direction or the other. By the time I'm told not to water them, the little plants are often waterlogged and growing mold on their leaves and roots. By the time the instruction to water them reaches me, they are dehydrated and on the brink of dying. It's frustrating to be growing a living thing up here and to watch it struggle, not to be able to take proper care of it. At one point, I post a picture of one of the zinnias on social media and get back criticism of my botany skills in return. "You're no Mark Watney," quips one wise-guy commenter, making reference to the stranded astronaut in the book and movie *The Martian*. Now it's personal.

Growing zinnias in space reminds me of gardening with my grandparents as a child.

I tell the payload ops director that I want to take over deciding when to water the flowers. That might seem like a small decision, but for NASA it's huge. Having to touch the plants and the medium they grow in with my bare hands would be a major change in protocol. The ground seems terrified that if I touch the plants and they have mold on them, the spores could infect me. The initial reaction I get is skeptical, but I'm convinced that the flowers are going to die unless I'm allowed to take care of them myself, as a gardener on Earth would do. But I finally get the okay.

It's hard to describe the feeling of watching the flowers come back from the brink of death. I've carried memories of the flowers I saw in the botanical gardens with my grandparents when I was a kid. Maybe because those weekends with them were a peaceful break, I associate flowers with my grandmother and her loving manner. I think about Laurel's violets that I kept in my office after her death. Once the zinnias are my personal project, it becomes incredibly important to me that they do well. I check on them as often as I can. One Friday I bring some of them down to the Russian segment and attach them to the table as a kind of centerpiece.

"Scott," Sergey says, a puzzled look on his face. "Why are you growing these flowers?"

"They're zinnias," I clarify.

"Why are you growing these zinnias?"

I explain that we are working toward being able to grow tomatoes one day, that this is one of the experiments we are doing to further our knowledge for long-term spaceflight. If a crew is going to go to Mars, they will want fresh food and won't have access to resupply rockets. If we can grow lettuce, maybe we can grow zinnias. If we can grow zinnias, maybe we can grow tomatoes, and tomatoes would provide real nutritional value to Mars travelers.

Sergey shakes his head. "Growing tomatoes is a waste. If you want to grow something you can eat, you should grow potatoes. You can live on potatoes. You can't live on tomatoes." The practical and simple Russian perspective has merit.

When I post the first picture of the healthy zinnias on social media, there is a huge explosion of interest—6 million people saw the photo. It's gratifying to see people respond strongly to something I've come to care about. And it proves that people are interested in what's going on in space if they can relate to what's happening.

To me, the success with the zinnias is a great example of how crew members will have to be able to make their own decisions if we ever go to Mars.

In late January, I pull on the brown fake-fur gorilla suit for the first time and stuff my head into the plasticky-smelling mask. I've decided what Space Gorilla's first adventure will be: I hide in Tim Kopra's crew quarters and wait for him to come along. When he opens the door, I pop out and scare him senseless. Then I float down to the Russian segment and show the cosmonauts, who all go nuts laughing. Space Gorilla is already spreading joy.

I decide it will be funny to float in front of the camera where mission control can see me in the suit without warning them first. On a calm Tuesday afternoon when not much is going on, I make my move. I put on the suit and then drift in front of the camera in the U.S. lab until I know I can be seen on the screen. Amiko sees it, but no one on the ground says anything. It's a letdown.

I've been thinking about ways to use Space Gorilla with kids—if he could grab their attention and make them laugh, maybe they would be interested enough to listen to me talk about space and the value of science, technology, engineering, and math. Tim Peake agrees to help me by costarring in a short video in which he is shown unpacking some cargo, only to find a stowaway gorilla that chases him up and down the U.S. lab to the song "Yakety Sax." The video goes viral and brings new attention to what we are doing on the space station.

Space Gorilla finally makes it to the ISS. February 2016.

On January 28, I lead a moment of silence for the crew of the space shuttle *Challenger*, which was lost thirty years ago today. The two Tims and I gather in the U.S. lab, where I say a few words honoring the memory of the crew and mentioning that their spirit lives on in our current achievements in space. I bow my head for a moment, and as I do, I can't help remembering the cold morning when my college roommate George and I watched the orbiter blow up over and over on his tiny TV. Thirty years, a lifetime ago. I couldn't have imagined I'd be where I am now.

One Sunday morning, I float over to the Russian segment and greet the cosmonauts while they are having breakfast.

"Scott!" Misha calls out to me with a mischievous smile on his face. "Do you know what today is?"

"Yes," I answer. "It's my birthday. February twenty-first."

"Happy birthday, Scott, but that's not it! We have only nine days left!"

Misha knows that I've avoided counting down this whole year. I'm surprised that the single digits have crept up on me, so it seems my strategy has worked. Nine days isn't long at all.

"Scott," Misha says with a note of celebration in his voice, "we did it!"

"Misha," I answer, "we had no choice!"

Sergey, Misha, and I will do a few Soyuz training sessions together so we will be ready for our descent. Misha, who will serve as flight engineer 1, needs to refresh his training for serving as Sergey's backup; it's been a long time.

We start packing our things and getting organized to leave. I have to figure out what is coming back with me on Soyuz—a small package of no more than a pound or so. A larger allotment of things can come back on Dragon later in the spring. I need to clean out my crew quarters thoroughly so it will be fresh for the next person. Because of the way stuff can float around in space, I have to clean the walls, ceiling, and floor. I have to take apart the small room and vacuum out the vents—those are especially gross, as they are covered with a year of dust. I also hide a plastic cockroach for my successor to find.

Amiko tells me she's had someone come by to check on the pool and hot tub at our house. She knows I have been thinking about how great it will be to jump in the pool as soon as I get home.

Often when I do interviews and press events from space, I'm asked what I miss about Earth. I have a few answers I always reach for that make sense in any context: I mention rain, spending time with my family, relaxing at home. Those are always true. But throughout the day, from moment to moment, I'm aware of missing all sorts of random things that don't even necessarily rise to the surface of my consciousness.

I miss cooking. I miss chopping fresh food, the smell vegetables give up when you first slice into them. I miss grocery stores, the shelves of bright colors and the glossy tile floors and the strangers wandering the aisles. I miss people. I miss the experience of meeting new people and getting to know them, learning about a life different from my own. I miss the sound of children playing, which always sounds the same no matter their language. I miss the sound of people talking and laughing in another room. I miss rooms. I miss doors and doorframes and the creak of wood floorboards when people walk around in old buildings. I miss sitting on my couch, sitting on a chair—resting after fighting gravity all day. I miss the rustle of papers, the flap of book pages turning. I miss drinking from a glass. I miss setting things down on a table and having them stay there. I miss the sudden chill of wind on my back, the warmth of sun on my face. I miss showers. I miss running water in all its forms: washing my face, washing my hands. I miss sleeping in a bed—the feel of sheets, the heft of a comforter, the welcoming curve of a pillow. I miss the surprise of the night sky and the variety of sunrises and sunsets on Earth.

I also think about what I'll miss about this place when I'm back on Earth. It's a strange feeling, this nostalgia in advance, nostalgia for things I'm still experiencing every day and that often, right now, annoy me. I know I will miss the friendship and camaraderie of the fourteen people I have flown with on this yearlong mission. I'll miss the view of Earth from the Cupola. I know I will miss the sense that I'm surviving by my wits, the sense that life-threatening challenges could come along and that I will rise to meet them, that every single thing I do is important, that every day could be my last.

Packing up to leave space is strange. A lot of stuff goes in the trash, which means stowing it in the Cygnus that will burn up in the atmosphere later this month. I throw out a lot of unused clothes—my challenge to myself to use as few clothes as possible has been a success, and there is a duffel bag's worth of T-shirts, sweatshirts, underwear, socks, and pants left over.

There is another thing I wanted to do that I haven't quite found the right time to do. I've been thinking about the whole arc of my life that brought me here and about what it meant to me to read *The Right Stuff* as a young man. I feel certain that I wouldn't have done any of the things I have if I hadn't read that book—if Tom Wolfe hadn't written it. On a quiet Saturday afternoon, I call Tom Wolfe to thank him. I got his number from an acquaintance, as I didn't know him. He sounds truly amazed to hear from me. I tell him we're passing over the Indian Ocean, how fast we're going, how our communication system works. We talk about books and about New York and about what I plan to do first when I get home (jump into my swimming pool). We agree to have lunch when I'm back on Earth, and that's now one of the things I'm looking forward to most.

On February 29, 2016, I hand over command of the International Space Station to Tim Kopra. Tomorrow I will leave the station and return to Earth.

24

On March 1, the six of us are gathered in the Russian segment, having another awkward photo op floating in front of the Soyuz hatch. When it's time, Sergey, Misha, and I each hug the Tims and Yuri and say our good-byes. They snap pictures of us as we float through the hatch. I know from experience that it's an odd feeling to say good-bye from that side, knowing that you will be staying behind in space while your friends return to Earth. After spending so much time together in such close quarters, we've now closed a door between us that won't open again.

Just before Sergey closes the hatch behind us, Misha turns and reaches through to touch the wall of the space station one last time. He gives it a pat, the way you'd pat a horse. I know he's thinking he might not be here again and he's feeling nostalgia for this place that has meant so much to him.

If the process of getting up to space is violent and uncomfortable, the process of coming back down is even more so. Descending in the Soyuz capsule is one of the most dangerous moments of this year, and it will be one of the most physically grueling. Earth's atmosphere is naturally resistant to objects entering from space. Moving at the high speed of orbit, any object will create friction with the air—enough friction that most objects simply burn up from the heat. This is a fact that generally works to our advantage, as it protects the planet from the many meteoroids and orbital debris that would otherwise rain down unexpectedly. And we take advantage of it when we fill visiting vehicles with trash and then set them loose to burn up in the atmosphere. But it's also what makes a return from space so difficult and dangerous. The three of us must survive a fall through the atmosphere that will create temperatures up to three thousand degrees and up to 4 g's of deceleration. The atmosphere seems designed to kill us, but the Soyuz capsule, and the procedures we go through, are designed to keep us alive.

The return to Earth will take about three and a half hours, with many steps we must get through successfully. After pushing away from the station, we will fire the engine to slow us slightly and ease our way into the upper layers of the atmosphere at just the right speed and angle to start our descent. If our approach is too steep, we could fall too fast and be killed by excessive heat or deceleration. If it's too shallow, we could skip off the surface of the atmosphere like a rock thrown at a still lake, only to later enter much more steeply, with catastrophic consequences. Assuming our deorbit burn goes as planned, the atmosphere will do most of the work of slowing us down, while the heat shield will (we hope) keep the temperatures from killing us, the parachute will (we hope) slow our descent once we are within 30,000 feet, and then the retrorockets will (we hope) fire to further slow our descent in the seconds before we hit the ground. Many things need to happen perfectly or we will be dead.

Sergey has already spent days stowing the cargo we will be bringing with us on the Soyuz—our small packages of personal items, water samples, blood and saliva for the human studies. We pack up some trash to be disposed of in the habitation module of the Soyuz, and I include the head of the gorilla suit, since I don't want to be held responsible for any future Space Gorilla antics. Most of the storage space in the capsule is devoted to things we hope we never have to use: the radio, compass, machete, and cold weather camping gear that comes with us in case we land off course and must wait for the rescue forces.

Because our cardiovascular systems have not had to work against gravity all this time, they have become weakened and we will suffer from symptoms of low blood pressure on our return to Earth. One of the things we do to counteract this is fluid loading—ingesting water and salt to try to increase our plasma volume before we return. The Russians and the Americans have different philosophies about the best fluid loading protocols. NASA gives us a range of options that include chicken broth, a combination of salt tablets and water, and Astro-Ade, a rehydration drink developed specifically for astronauts. The Russians prefer more salt and less liquid, in part because they prefer not to use the diaper during reentry. Having figured out what worked for me on my previous flights, I stick to drinking lots of water and wearing the diaper.

I struggle into my Sokol suit, which is even harder to get into here than it was in Baikonur, where gravity kept things still and I had suit technicians to help me.

We float into the center section of the Soyuz, the descent capsule, one by one, and struggle into our seats. We sit with our knees pressed up to our chests.

We are in the seat liners that were custom molded to fit our bodies, and they are more important now than they were on launch day. We will go from 17,500 miles per hour to a hard zero in less than thirty minutes, and the seats, along with many other parts of the Soyuz, must work as designed to keep us on the winning side of a battle against the forces of nature. We strap ourselves in as best we can using the five-point restraints, easier said than done when the straps are floating around us and any tiny force pushes us away from the seats. It's hard to get secured very tightly, but once we are hurtling toward Earth, the full force of gravity will crush us down into our seats, making it easier to fully tighten our straps.

A command from mission control in Moscow opens the hooks that hold the Soyuz to the ISS, and soon after, spring-force plungers nudge us away from the station. Both of these processes are so gentle that we don't feel or hear them. We are now moving a couple of inches per second relative to the station, though still in orbit with it. Once we are a safe distance away, we use the Soyuz thrusters to push us farther from the ISS.

Now there is more waiting. We don't talk much. This squashed position creates excruciating pain in my knees, as it always has, and it's warm in here. A cooling fan runs to circulate air within our suits, a low comforting whirr, but it's not enough.

I find it hard to stay awake. I don't know if I'm tired just from today or from the whole year. Sometimes you don't feel how exhausting something has been until it's over and you allow yourself to stop ignoring it. I look over at Sergey and Misha, and their eyes are closed. I close mine, too. The sun rises; forty-five minutes later, the sun sets.

When we get word from the ground that it's time for the deorbit burn, we are instantly, completely awake. It's important to get this part right. Sergey and Misha execute the burn perfectly, a four-and-a-half-minute firing of the braking rockets, which will slow the Soyuz by 300 miles per hour. We are now in a twenty-five-minute free fall before we slam into Earth's atmosphere.

When it's time to separate the crew module—the tiny, cone-shaped capsule we are sitting in—from the rest of the Soyuz, we hold our breaths. The three modules are exploded apart. Pieces of the habitation module and instrumentation compartment fly by the windows, some of them striking the sides of our spacecraft. None of us mentions it, but we all know that it was at this point in a Soyuz descent in 1971 that three cosmonauts lost their lives. A valve between the crew module and the orbital module opened during separation, depressurizing the cabin and suffocating the crew. Misha, Sergey, and I wear pressure suits that would protect us in the case of a similar accident, but this moment in the descent sequence is still one we are glad to put behind us.

We feel gravity begin to return, first slowly, then with a vengeance. Soon everything is oddly heavy, too heavy—our manuals, our arms, our heads. My watch feels heavy on my wrist, and breathing gets harder as the g forces clamp down on my trachea. I extend my head up as I struggle to breathe. We are falling at a thousand feet per second. The capsule heats up, and flaming pieces of the heat shield fly by the window as it's scorched black.

We hear the wind noise building as the thick air of the atmosphere rushes past the capsule, a sign that the parachute will soon be deployed. This is the only part of reentry that is completely automated, and we concentrate on the monitor, waiting for the indicator light to show that it worked. It won't be long, maybe only a second or two, before we feel the jerk of the parachute, but we watch anyway. Everything now depends on one parachute, manufactured in an aging facility outside Moscow by similarly aging workers using quality standards inherited from the Soviet space program. After all I've experienced this year—the long days, the grueling spacewalks, living through the missed birthdays and celebrations, the struggles personal and professional—everything depends on that parachute. We are falling at the speed of sound. We fall and wait and watch.

The chute catches us with a jerk, rolling and buffeting our capsule crazily through the sky. I've heard this experience compared to a train accident followed by a car accident followed by falling off your bike. I've described it myself as the sensation of going over Niagara Falls in a barrel, while the barrel is on fire. In the wrong frame of mind this would be terrifying, and from what I've heard, some people who have experienced it have been terrified. But I love it. As soon as you realize you're not going to die, it's the most fun you'll ever have in your life—like a carnival ride on steroids.

Although the parachute softens our landing and keeps us from crashing into the Earth at a deadly speed, touching down is still a jarring end to our year in space. March 2, 2016.

Misha's checklist comes loose from its tether and flies at my head. I reach up and grab it out of the air left-handed. The three of us look at one another with amazement.

"Left-handed Super Bowl catch!" I shout, then quickly realize Sergey and Misha might not know what the Super Bowl is.

After all the tumult of the descent, the minutes we spend drifting at the whim of the parachute are oddly calm. Later I will see a photograph taken of our Soyuz dangling under the white-and-orange parachute against the backdrop of a fluffy blanket of clouds. The heat shield is jettisoned, pulling off the burned window coverings. Sunlight streams in the window at my elbow as we watch the ground come closer and closer.

From their position in helicopters nearby, the rescue forces count down to us the distance to go until landing.

"Open your mouth," a voice reminds us in Russian. If we don't keep our tongues away from our teeth, we could bite them off on impact. When we are only five meters (16.4 feet) from the ground, the retro rockets fire for the "soft" landing (this is what it's called, but I know from experience that the landing is anything but soft). I feel the hard crack of hitting the Earth in my spine. My head bounces and slams into the seat, the sensation of a car accident. We are down. We have landed with the hatch pointing straight up rather than on one side, which is rare. We will wait a few minutes longer than usual while the rescue crew brings a ladder to extract us from the burned capsule.

When the hatch opens, the Soyuz fills with the rich smell of air and the bracing cold of winter. It smells fantastic. We bump fists.

After Sergey gets out of the capsule, I'm surprised to find that I can unstrap myself, pull myself out of my seat, and reach the hatch overhead, despite the fact that gravity feels like a crushing force. With the help of the rescue crew, I pull myself entirely out of the capsule to sit on the edge of the hatch and take in the landscape all around. The sight of so many people—maybe a couple hundred—is startling. It feels indescribably strange to see more than a handful of people at a time, and the sight is overwhelming.

I pump my fist in the air. I breathe, and the air is rich with the fantastic scent of grass combined with the unmistakable aroma of charred Soyuz, like the sweet smell of honeysuckle I remember from childhood. The Russian space agency insists on having the rescue crew help us down from the capsule and deposit us into nearby camp chairs for examination by doctors and nurses. We follow the Russians' rules when we travel with them, but I wish they would let me walk away from the landing. I feel sure I could.

I give a thumbs-up to our recovery crew. The cold air on my face feels amazing. It is so good to be back on Earth. March 2, 2016.

The ground crew carries me from the landing site to the medical tent for a checkup. Reentering Earth's gravity is hard on a body after a long time in space. March 2, 2016.

My flight surgeon Steve Gilmore is there, and I'm reminded of what his medical care and friendship have meant to me. Over the years, he and other flight surgeons have worked to keep me on flight status and kept me flying safely. I notice Chris Cassidy, the chief astronaut, and my friend Joel Montalbano, the deputy ISS program manager. Near Sergey and Misha, I recognize Sergey's father and Valery Korzun, both former cosmonauts. In the distance, I see the rescue force troops, some of whom I had first met in Russia in 2000 during winter survival training and whose dedication I have come to appreciate and rely on. I notice Misha smiling and waving at them, and

I know he's thinking of his father, who was once one of them. Chris hands me a satellite phone. I dial Amiko's cell—she's at mission control in Houston along with my daughter Samantha, my brother, and close friends watching the live feed on the huge screens. Charlotte watched with her mom from their home in Virginia.

"How was it?" Amiko asks.

"It was totally medieval," I say. "But effective." I tell her I feel fine.

If I were on the first crew to reach the surface of Mars, just now touching down on the red planet after a yearlong journey and a wild, hot descent through its atmosphere, I feel like I would be able to do what needed to be done. Since Mars's gravity is lower than Earth's, it would be easier to function, which would definitely help. One of the most important questions of my mission has been a simple yes or no: Could you do work on Mars? I wouldn't want to have to build a habitat or hike ten miles, but I know I could take care of myself and others in an emergency, and that feels like a triumph.

I tell Amiko I'll see her soon, and for the first time in a year, that's true.

EPILOGUE

LIFE ON EARTH

I'VE BEEN ASKED often what we learned from my year in space. I think sometimes people want to hear about one profound scientific discovery or insight, something that struck me (or the scientists on the ground) like a cosmic ray through my retina at some climactic moment during my mission. I don't have anything like that to offer. The mission that I prepared for was, for the most part, the mission I flew. The data is still being analyzed as I write this, and the scientists are excited about what they are seeing so far. The genetic differences between my brother and me from this year could unlock new knowledge, not only about what space-flight does to our bodies but also about how we age here on Earth.

Results and scientific papers will continue to emerge over years and decades based on the four hundred experiments we conducted over the year. Misha and I were a sample size of only two—we need to see many more astronauts stay in space for longer periods of time before we can draw conclusions about what we experienced. I do feel as though I've made discoveries—it's just that those discoveries can't entirely be separated from what I've learned from my other missions in space, other periods of my life, other challenges, other lessons.

As much as I worked on scientific experiments, I think I

learned at least as much about practical issues of how to conduct a long-range exploration mission. This is what crew members on ISS are always doing—we are not just solving problems and trying to make things better for our own spaceflights, but also studying how to make things better for the future. And the larger struggles of my mission—most notably, CO_2 management and upkeep of the Seedra—will have a larger impact on future missions on the space station and future space vehicles. NASA has agreed to manage CO_2 at a much lower target level, and better versions of carbon dioxide scrubbers are being developed that will one day replace the Seedra and make life better for future space travelers.

Personally, I've learned that nothing feels as amazing as water. The night my plane landed in Houston and I finally got to go home, I did exactly what I'd been saying I would do all along: I walked in the front door, walked out the back door, and jumped into my swimming pool, still in my flight suit. The sensation of being immersed in water for the first time in a year is impossible to describe. I'll never take water for granted again. Misha says he feels the same way.

I've been assigned to a spaceflight or in training for one practically nonstop since 1999. It will be an adjustment to no longer be planning my life this way. I have to reflect on what I've learned.

I've learned that I can be really calm in bad situations. I've known this about myself since I was a kid, but it has definitely been reinforced.

I've learned to better compartmentalize, which doesn't mean forgetting about feelings but instead means focusing on the things I can control and ignoring what I can't.

I've learned from watching my mother train to become a police officer that small steps add up to giant leaps.

I've learned how important it is to sit and eat with other people. While I was in space, I saw on TV one day a scene of people sitting down to eat a meal together. The sight moved me with an unexpected yearning. I suddenly longed to sit at a table with my family, just like the people on the screen, gravity holding a freshly cooked meal on the table's surface so we could enjoy it, gravity holding us in our seats so we could rest. I had asked Amiko to buy a dining room table; she did, and sent me a picture of it. Two days after landing, I was sitting at the head of the new table, a beautiful meal my friend Tilman had sent over spread out on it, my family gathered around me. It was just how I'd pictured it.

I've learned that most problems aren't rocket science, but when they are rocket science, you should ask a rocket scientist. In other words, I've learned to seek advice and counsel and to listen to experts. I've learned that an achievement that seems to have been accomplished by one person probably has hundreds, maybe even thousands, of people's minds and work behind it, and I've learned that it's a privilege to be the embodiment of that work.

I've learned that a year in space contains a lot of contradictions. A year away from someone you love both strains the relationship and strengthens it in new ways. I've learned that climbing into a rocket that may kill me is both a confrontation of mortality and an adventure that makes me feel more alive than anything else I've ever experienced. I've learned that this moment in American spaceflight is a crossroads where we can either renew our commitment to push farther out, to build on our successes, to keep doing harder and harder things—or else lower our sights and compromise our goals.

I've learned that grass smells great and wind feels amazing

and rain is a miracle. I will try to remember how magical these things are for the rest of my life.

I've learned that my daughters are remarkable and incredibly resilient people, and that I have missed a piece of each of their lives that I can never get back.

I've learned that following the news from space can make Earth seem like a swirl of chaos and conflict, and that seeing the environmental damage caused by humans is heartbreaking. I've also learned that our planet is the most beautiful thing I've ever seen and that we're lucky to have it.

I've learned a new empathy for other people, including people I don't know and people I disagree with. I've started letting people know I appreciate them, which can sometimes freak them out at first. It's a bit out of character. But it's something I'm glad to have gained and hope to keep.

I will continue to participate in the Twins Study as Mark and I age. Science is a slow-moving process, and it may be years before any great understanding or breakthrough is reached from the data. This doesn't particularly bother me—I will leave the science up to the scientists. For me, it's worth it to have contributed to advancing human knowledge, even if it's only a step on a much longer journey.

I've been traveling the country and the world talking about my experiences in space. It's gratifying to see how curious people are about my mission, how much children instinctively feel the excitement and wonder of spaceflight, and how many people think, as I do, that Mars is the next step.

In the summer after I returned, my father was diagnosed with throat cancer and was receiving radiation therapy. In October, he became much more ill. One evening, Amiko got a phone call from him, which wasn't unusual. He had depended on her support a great deal while I was in space, and they had continued to talk often. But that day, he didn't want anything in particular.

"I just wanted to let you know how much I love you, sweetheart," he told her. "I'm just so glad you and Scott have each other. You've accomplished so much together, and all the stuff you've been through—it was all worth it." Amiko thought this was out of character for him, but she said he sounded much better than he had in a while. A few days later, he took a turn for the worse, and while Mark, Amiko, and I were all out of the country, he died in the intensive care unit with my daughter Samantha by his side, four and a half years after my mother's death. I was grateful Samantha could be there with him.

I'm convinced he lived to see my mission through and to celebrate my return. It was a big deal to him to support Mark and me and to celebrate our accomplishments, and he was proudest of all of his granddaughters, whom he adored. Like most people, he had mellowed with age, and we had a much-improved relationship toward the end of his life.

In my computer, I have a file of all the images my crewmates and I took on the International Space Station during the time I was there. When I'm trying to remember some detail from the mission, sometimes I click through them. It can be overwhelming, because there are so many of them—half a million—but often a picture of a specific person on a specific day will bring back a flood of sense memory, and I will suddenly remember the smell of the space station, or the laughter of my crewmates, or the texture of the quilted walls inside my CQ.

One image that doesn't exist in my computer but that I will always remember is the view from the Soyuz window as Sergey, Misha, and I backed away from the International Space Station. As well as I know the inside of the station, I've seen the outside only a handful of times. It's a strange sight, glinting in the reflected sunlight, as long as a football field, its solar arrays spread out more than half an acre. It's a completely unique structure, assembled by spacewalkers flying around the Earth at 17,500 miles per hour in a vacuum, in extremes of temperature of plus and minus 270 degrees, the work of fifteen different countries over eighteen years, thousands of people speaking different languages and using different engineering methods and standards. In some cases the station's modules never touched one another while on Earth, but they all fit together perfectly in space.

As we backed away, I knew I would never see it again, this place where I'd spent more than five hundred days of my life. We won't have a space station like this again in my lifetime, and I will always be grateful for the part I've played in its life. In a world of compromise and uncertainty, the ISS is a triumph of engineering and cooperation. Putting this space station into orbit—making it work and keeping it working—is the hardest thing that human beings have ever done, and it stands as proof that when we set our minds to something hard, when we work together, we can do anything, including solving our problems here on Earth.

I also know that if we want to go to Mars, it will be very, very difficult, it will cost a great deal of money, and it may likely cost human lives. But I know now that if we decide to do it, we can.

ACKNOWLEDGMENTS

Amiko said to me once, "Teamwork makes the dream work," and spaceflight is the biggest team sport there is, so spending any amount of time in space takes the support and collaboration of thousands of people. From the instructors who train us to the flight controllers and flight directors working in mission control to my friends and family keeping me connected to my life on Earth—there isn't enough space in this book to thank them all, so one collective "thank you" will have to suffice.

Above all, I have to recognize my partner—and now wife—Amiko Kauderer. I hope the pages of this book make clear what it meant to me that she was with me day by day throughout this journey, experiencing together its challenges and triumphs and its highs and lows. I've tried to express what a crucial role she's played in this mission's success, but words can never express the role she has played in my life these last eight years. Thank you, Amiko.

My kids, Samantha and Charlotte, have sacrificed much for their dad, from missed birthdays and holidays to the general disruption of their lives, accepting the inherent risks of spaceflight and sharing their dad with the world. They were brave, adaptable, and resilient. I appreciate and am proud of how you handled it all with strength and grace. Thank you.

My brother, Mark, has been by my side since birth, challenging and supporting me throughout our lives. Having also flown in space, he understood the thrill, the trials, and the hardships of this journey. His support and counsel I've come to rely on and much appreciate. Thank you.

My parents endured the emotional toll of watching their sons launch into space and awaiting our safe return to Earth—a total of seven times for my mother, Patricia, and eight times for my father, Richard. Thank you to my mother also for showing me by her example what it took to achieve a lofty goal.

My ex-wife, Leslie, lent her willing support, accepting the role of a full-time single parent, ensuring our daughters were safe and cared for back on Earth each time I went to work off the planet. Thank you.

My collaborator on the adult version of *Endurance*, Margaret Lazarus Dean, for her insight and help on this version.

My collaborator Emily Easton, editor and adapter of this version of *Endurance*, for putting my memoir into a version acceptable for young readers—a challenge since I'm a former navy guy and sometimes speak (and write) like a sailor.

And finally, I have to thank Tom Wolfe for his early inspiration. I truly believe if an eighteen-year-old me had not read his book *The Right Stuff*, there would be no *Endurance*.

HOW TO SPEAK LIKE A PILOT

bingo: When a jet has run out of fuel

bogey: Unidentified aircraft, usually assumed to be an enemy

bolter: When a pilot attempts to land on a carrier but the aircraft's hook doesn't catch the arresting wire, forcing the pilot to take off again

Bravo Zulu: Congratulating a pilot on a good job

call the ball: When a pilot lines up to land on a carrier deck by visually lining up with the landing system lights

G-LOC: When g's cause a pilot to lose consciousness (LOC = loss of consciousness)

goo: Bad weather that impacts visibility in the sky

green bag: Flight suit a Navy pilot wears; also called a zoombag

G suit: Flight pants that fill with compressed air during high g's to keep blood from pooling in the legs and feet. This helps to prevent a pilot from losing consciousness. Also called speed jeans.

hook slap: When an aircraft's tailhook hits the back of a carrier's flight deck in a landing attempt

merge: The airspace where aircraft flying toward each other in a dogfight first make contact

punch out: When a pilot ejects from a plane

ready room: Room on an aircraft carrier where on-duty pilots
wait and prepare for flight and combat

roll 'em: Themed movie night in a squadron's ready room,
complete with snacks from the ship's store

tailhooker: Pilot who has been qualified to land on a carrier

touch-and-go landing: Landing on a runway and taking off
again without stopping—a practice maneuver for a new pilot

trick or treat: Last attempt to land on a carrier before having to
give up and return to the airfield

wingman: In a two-plane group, the second pilot who protects
the back of the lead aircraft

HOW TO SPEAK LIKE AN ASTRONAUT

affirmative: More formal way of saying yes

AOS (Acquisition of Signal): Radio signal is being received

CAPCOM (capsule communication): Point of contact in mission control for astronauts in space

confirm: Agreement that a statement is accurate

control: Short for ground control. Often refers to the Mission Control Center in Houston.

copy: Message received and understood

deploy: Put a piece of equipment into use

downlink: Connect a radio signal from the shuttle to mission control

LOS: Abbreviation for Loss of (radio) Signal

negative: More formal way of saying no

negative copy: Message was not heard or understood

over: When a person has finished talking and it is the other person's turn to speak

uplink: Connect a radio signal from mission control to a spacecraft

you have a go for . . . : Mission control has approved a particular action

A GLOSSARY OF SPACE TERMS

AU: Astronomical Unit, or the mean distance between the Earth and the Sun—92,955,807 miles (149,597,870 km)

blackout (radio): Temporary loss of radio communication. This happens when a spacecraft reenters the Earth's atmosphere and an ionized sheath of plasma forms around the craft.

burn: Combustion action in rockets. A spacecraft launches into space through a sequence of rocket burns.

cosmonaut: Russian term for an astronaut

countdown: Reverse time count, measuring the hours, minutes, and seconds left before a spacecraft or rocket launches

cutoff: Stopping a process abruptly, such as shutting off the fuel to a rocket during launch

decay: When an object in orbit slows due to **drag**, causing it to spiral back down into the Earth's atmosphere, where it will eventually disintegrate or burn up

delta V: Difference or change in velocity, or speed

drag: Resistance caused by a gas or liquid to an object moving through it. This action causes the object to slow down.

eclipse: When one celestial body passes in front of another and blocks it from view, either partially or totally

escape velocity: Speed needed to escape from a given point in a gravitational field. The velocity needed to escape from the Earth's surface is 6.95 miles per second (11.2 km per sec).

EVA (Extravehicular Activity): Spacewalk

flyby: Spaceflight past a heavenly body without orbiting

FOV: Field of View

g: Symbol for the acceleration of a freely moving body due to gravity at the surface of the Earth; alternatively, 1 g

go or no-go: Latest point at which a decision to proceed with a mission or an action can be made

gravity: Force responsible for the mutual attraction of separate masses

hatch: Door in space that is sealed to protect the artificial atmosphere within the spacecraft

heat shield: Device that protects people and equipment within a spacecraft from extreme heat, such as the heat encountered during reentry into Earth's atmosphere

launch window: Interval of time during which a space vehicle can be launched to accomplish a given mission, such as a flight to Venus or Mars

LEO (Low Earth Orbit): 1,200 miles (2,000 km) above sea level. Other than the Apollo missions to the moon, all human spaceflight has taken place in LEO.

liftoff: Start of a rocket's flight from its launch pad; also called blastoff

light speed: Distance light travels in one second—186,282 miles per second (299,792 km per second)

light-year: Distance light travels in one year—approximately 5.88 trillion miles (9.46 trillion km)

LT: Launch Time

mach: Ratio of the speed of a vehicle (or of a liquid or gas) to the local speed of sound

MEO (Medium Earth Orbit): Area between 1,243 miles (2,000 km) above sea level and 12,552 miles (20,200 km) above sea level, mostly used by satellites for GPS navigation, communication, and space science

MMU (Manned Maneuvering Unit): Portable jet-pack device that astronauts use to move through space outside of the spacecraft

module: Unit or compartment of a spacecraft or space station. Many modules linked together form the structure of the International Space Station.

NASA: National Aeronautics and Space Administration

payload: Cargo carried by a spacecraft

PLSS: Portable Life Support System

probe: Unmanned instrumented vehicle sent into space to gather information

radar: System or technique for detecting the position, motion, and nature of a remote object by means of radio waves reflected from its surface

RE: Unit of distance equal to the radius of the Earth—3,959 miles (6,371 km)

reentry: Descent into Earth's atmosphere from space

rendezvous: Place of meeting at a given time; for example, a spaceship with a space station

retro-rocket: Rocket fired to reduce the speed of a spacecraft

RLV: Reusable Launch Vehicle

Roscosmos: Shortened name of the Roscosmos State

Corporation for Space Activities, the Russian government agency responsible for spaceflight programs

RV: Reentry Vehicle

satellite: Any body, natural or artificial, in orbit around a planet. The term is used most often to describe moons and spacecraft.

scrub: Postpone the launch of a spacecraft or rocket due to poor weather conditions or equipment malfunction

throttle: Decrease the supply of propellant/fuel to an engine, reducing **thrust**. Liquid propellant rocket engines can be throttled; solid rocket motors cannot.

thrust: Force that propels a rocket or spacecraft measured in pounds, kilograms, or newtons

trajectory: Flight path of a projectile, missile, rocket, or satellite

universe: All matter and energy, including Earth, the solar system, the galaxies and everything contained within them, and the contents of intergalactic space, all together as one whole

uplink: Radio signal transmitted to a spacecraft from Earth

UTC (Coordinated Universal Time): Worldwide scientific standard of timekeeping, based on atomic clocks that are accurate to within microseconds. It is based on the time in Greenwich, England. UTC is the time zone used to mark time on the ISS.

zero gravity: Condition in which gravity appears to be absent. Zero gravity occurs when gravitational forces are balanced by the acceleration of a body in orbit or free fall.

PHOTO CREDITS

Key: t—top, b—bottom, c—center, l—left, r—right

Mark Kelly: 233 (r); Scott Kelly: vi, 6, 13, 16, 24, 39, 43, 48, 55, 60, 67, 272; Nathan Koga: iv–v; NASA: 2, 18, 19, 30, 63, 70, 73, 78, 83, 88, 91, 93, 98, 103, 107, 117, 121, 123, 174, 184, 190, 199, 205, 218, 222, 229, 232, 233 (l), 252, 262–263, 270, 293; NASA/James Blair: 141; NASA/Carla Cioffi: 119; NASA/Bill Ingalls: 129, 134, 136, 145, 150, 155, 212, 290, 292; NASA/Scott Kelly: 75, 163, 165, 167, 170, 182, 193, 265, 277, 280; NASA/Kjell Lindgren: 248; NASA/George Shelton: 110; NASA/Bill Stafford: 239; NASA/Terry Virts: 160, 178; NASA/Victor Zelemtsov: 138, 140, 149; National Archives photo no. 330-CFD-DF-SN-91–05830: 36; Star-Ledger Photographs © *The Star-Ledger*, Newark, NJ: 12 (l, r); SUNY Maritime College: 31; Jerry P. Tarnoff: 15; U.S. Navy/Mass Communication Specialist 2nd Class Todd Frantom: 34; U.S. Navy/VF-143—The World Famous Pukin' Dogs: 52–53.

PHOTO INSERT

Scott Kelly: 2 (t, b), 3 (b), 7 (tl); NASA: 1 (t, b), 4 (t, b), 5 (t, b), 6 (t, b), 8 (t, b), 11 (b), 12 (t, b), 13 (t), 14 (t); NASA/Carla Cioffi: 7 (b); NASA/Bill Ingalls: 9 (t, b), 10 (t, b), 14 (b), 15 (b); NASA/Scott Kelly: 11 (t), 13 (b), 15 (t); U.S. Navy: 3 (t); NASA/Robert Markowitz: 16; NASA/Stephanie Stoll: 7 (tr).

INDEX

ABOUT THE AUTHOR

Scott Kelly is a NASA astronaut best known for spending a record-breaking year in space. He is a former U.S. Navy fighter pilot, test pilot, and veteran of four spaceflights. Kelly commanded the space shuttle *Endeavour* in 2007 and twice commanded the International Space Station. He resides in Houston, Texas. You can follow him on Facebook at NASA Astronaut Scott Kelly, and on Instagram and Twitter at @StationCDRKelly.